Learn SAP SD in 1 Day

By Krishna Rungta

Table Of Content

Chapter 1: Create Customer Master Data: SAP XD01

Background

Customer Master is **Primary** master data in SAP SD. To create Customer Master we need Account Group. **Account Group:** Account Group is accumulation of similar accounts. The master records in the CUSTOMER hierarchy are controlled by their ACCOUNT GROUPS.

1. It determines Optional, Mandatory and Not Requires information for Customer.

2. Partner Functions is also linked with Account Group.

3. Account Group defines the way, numbers are assigned to customer.

T-Code for Create Customer master - FD01 / XD01 / VD01

- FD01- Company code level & data will be stored in tables KNA1 and KNB1.

- XD01- Include sales area & data will be stored in tables KNA1, KNB1 and KNVV (With company code data).

- VD01 - Include sales area & data will be stored in tables KNA1, KNB1 and KNVV (w/o Company code data).

We will use here XD01 for Customer Master Creation.

Step 1 - Enter T-Code XD01 in Command field.

Step 2 - Enter the detail in Address Tab screen as below-

1. Enter the title and name of customer.

2. Enter search term, for searching customer.

3. Enter Street / House Number.

4. Enter District / Postal code / City / Country / Region.

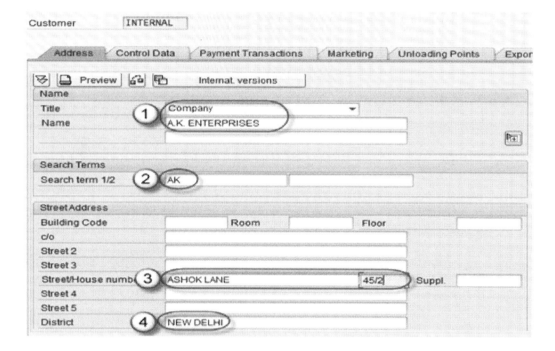

Step 3 - Enter Data in Control Data Tab Screen Field

1. Enter Tax Number

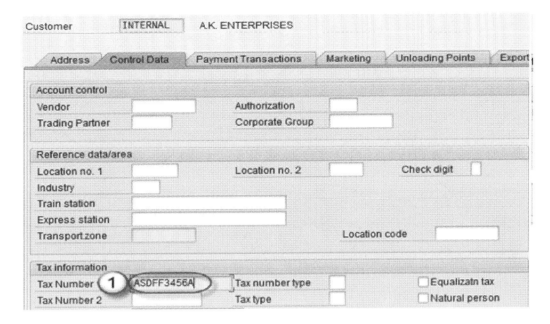

Step 4 - Enter Data on Payment Transactions tab.

1. Click on the Payment Transaction tab.

2. Enter Bank City / Bank Key / Bank Account / Account Holder Name.

3. To enter more detail about bank, click on Bank Data Button.

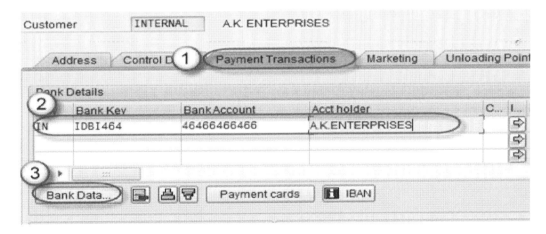

After Click on Bank data Button ,below screen appear-

1. Enter bank name / region

2. Enter City

3. Enter Swift Code

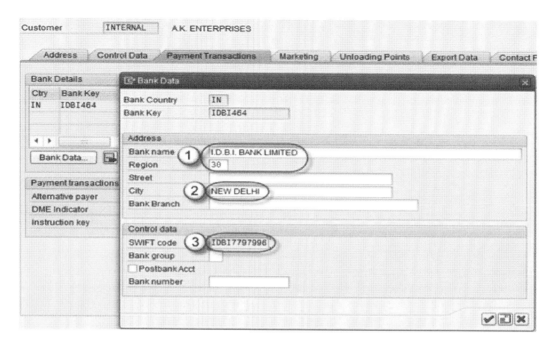

Click on Tick Button.

Step 5 - Enter sales area data-

1. Click on sales area button on application tool bar.

2. Enter Customer pricing procedure / Shipping data / Partner functions.

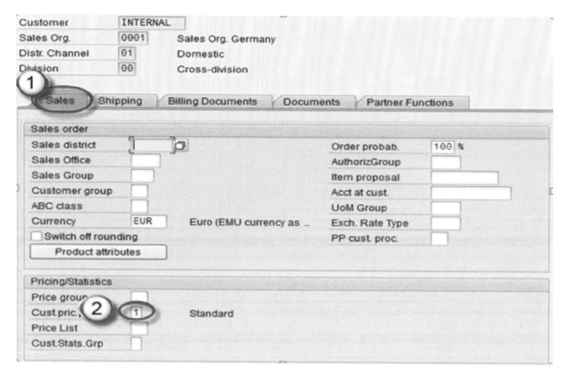

Step 6 - Save the record.

Click on Save Button.

Customer Will be created with Customer number.

☑ Customer 0000000612 has been created for company code 0001 sales area 0001 01 00

Main Transaction Codes in a Customer Master

Transaction Codes	Description
XD01, XD02, XD03	Used to create/change/display customer centrally
VD01,VD02,VD03	Used to create/change/display customer sales area
FD01,FD02,FD03	Used to create/change/display customer company code
XD04	Display change documents
XD05	Display change documentsUsed to block Customer – Global, order, delivery, billing, sales area, etc.
XD06	Used for deletion
XD07	Change Account Group
VAP1	Create Contact Person

Key tables in Customer Master

Table Name	Description
KNA1	General Information
KNB1	Company Code
KNVV	Sales Area
KNBK	Bank Data
VCNUM	Credit Card
VCKUN	Credit Card Assignment
MASSKNVK	General Data in Customer Master
KNVK	Contact Person
KNVP	Partner Functions
MASSKNVK	Contact Partner
MASSKNVD	Rrecord sales request form
KNVL	Customer Master Licenses
KNVI	Tax Indicator

KNVA	Unloading Points
KNAS	VAT registration numbers general section

Chapter 2: Create Number Range & Assign to Account Group XDN1

In this tutorial, we will learn How to Create Number Range & Assign Number Range to Customer Accounts groups

Step 1) Customer Number Range and Assignment

Enter T-Code XDN1 in command bar and press enter.

Step 2)

We now create Customer Number Ranges. Click on Intervals Create Button.

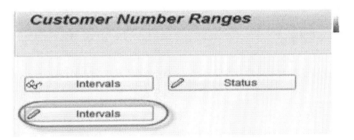

Step 3)

A screen name Maintain Number Range Intervals appear.

Click on +Interval Button.

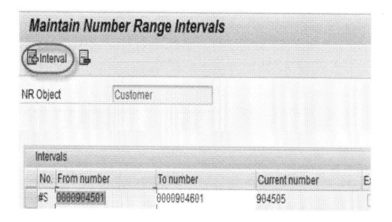

Step 4)

Screens as below appear.

1. Give the number range.

2. Click on save button.

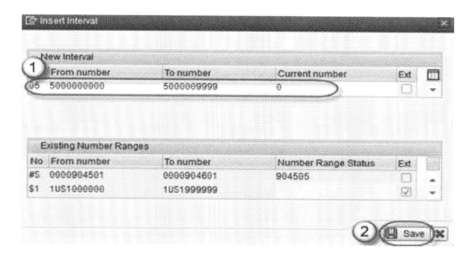

A message display "The changes were saved".

Step 5) Assign Number Range to Customer Accounts groups

Enter T-Code -OBAR in Command Bar.

1. Assign Number range to Customer Account Group.

2. Save the screen.

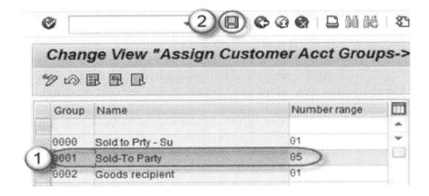

A message display "The changes were saved".

Chapter 3: How to Create Partner Function & Partner Determination: SAP VOPAN

What is Partner Function?

Partner function is two-character identification key that describes the people and organization with whom you do the business, and who are therefore involved in transaction. Here is some standard Partner Function for customer-

1. Sold-to party

2. Ship-to party

3. Bill-to party

4. Payer

What is Partner Determination?

The Partner and business partner term in SAP SD refers to parties with whom you do business. Each business partner has specific role. E.g. Sold-to party - Business Partner who order the goods / Services. The Partner Determination can be done in three steps-

Step 1 Define Partner Function

Step 2 Create Partner Determination procedure by grouping Partner function.

Step 3 Assign the partner determination procedure to respective partner object.

Step 1 - Define Partner Function:

1. Enter T-Code VOPAN in Command Bar.

2. Select Customer Master Partner Object

3. Click on Change Button, Partner Determination Procedure Screen appear.

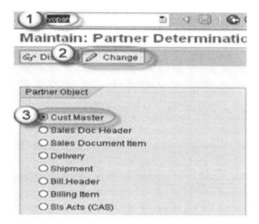

1. Click On New Entries Button.

2. Enter Partner Determination Procedure and name.

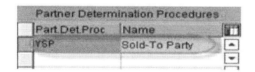

3. Double click on Partner Function node - Screen as below appear.

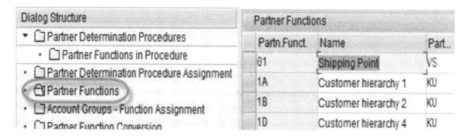

4. Click on New Entries New Entries Button.

5. Enter Partner Function Detail

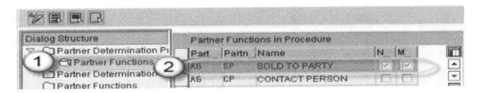

Enter Partner Function / Name / Partner Type.

Field Name	Desc
Partner Function	Two-character unique identifier for each partner function.
Name	A meaningful description for this partner function.
Partner Type	It tells whether the partner function is for a customer (KU), a vendor (LI), a contact person (AP), and so on.

Step 2 - Partner Determination procedure by grouping Partner function.

1. Click on Partner Function in procedure node.

2. Enter Partner Det. Procedure / Partner function / Name.

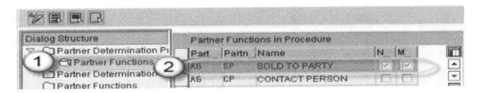

Step 3 - Assign the partner determination procedure to respective partner object. We are creating partner function for customer, so here partner object is customer and assign to Account Group.

Partner Object	Assign to
Customer	Account Group

Sales Document Header	Sales Document Type
Sales Document Item	Item category Type
Delivery Header	Delivery Document Type
Shipment Header	Shipment Document Type
Billing Header	Billing Document Type
Billing Item	Billing Item Category type
Contact	Contact type

1. Click on Account groups - Function Node and click on New entries Button.

2. Enter Partner function / Name / Account Group / Name.

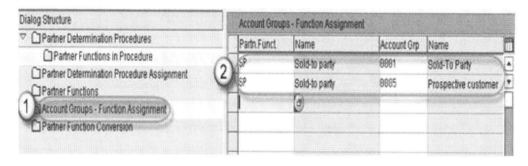

Click on Save Button ⊞ to save partner Function.

Chapter 4: How to Create Material Stock

Background

Their are more then one Tcode for create Material Stock .

1. MB1C (Other Goods Receipts) for opening balance creation of material.

2. MIGO (used for Issue / Transfer / Receipt of material).

We use here MB1C Tcode to Create Material Stock as opening balance.

Step-1.

1. Enter Tcode MB1C in command field.

2. Enter Movement Type 561 , Plant & Storage location.

click Enter Button.

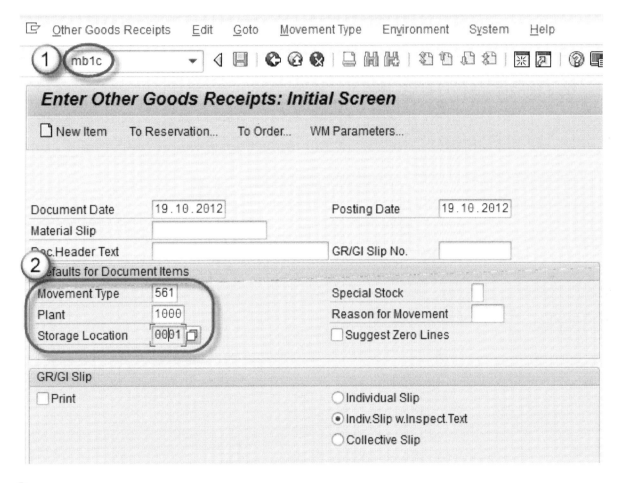

Step-2

After enter on above screen ,item screen as below appear-

- Enter Material code for which we need to create stock.

- Enter Quantity of material for stock creation.

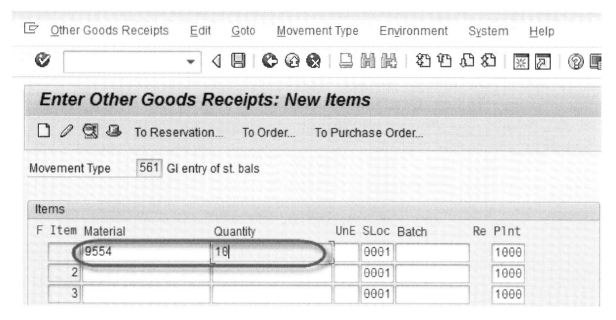

Step-3

click on save 🖫 button .

A message "Document 5000021944 posted" displayed.

☑ Document 5000021944 posted

Chapter 5: How to Create Customer Material Info Record

Background:

Sometimes, customer refers to a material with a layman name(rather than technical name) in purchase order .Hence there is a need to map customer material name with our material code, this process is called Customer Material Info Record.

T-Code is - VD51 (Create) / VD52 (Change) / VD53 (Display)

Step-1

1. Enter T-Code VD51 in command bar .

2. Enter customer code / sales organization / distribution channel.

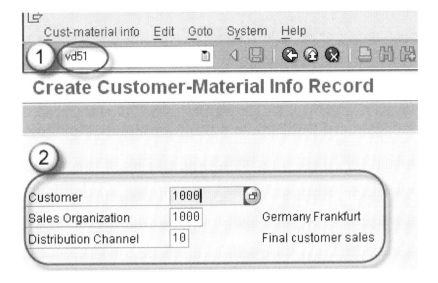

Press Enter Button, a next screen will appear.

Step-2

1. Enter material no. and customer material .

2. Click on Save Button.

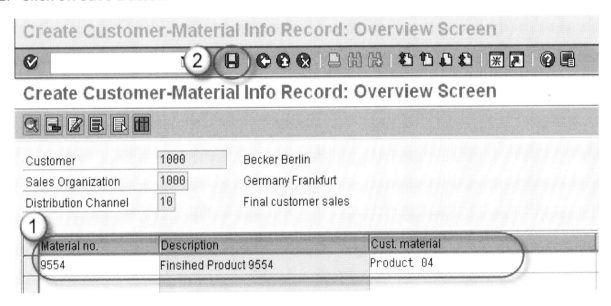

A Message " Customer-Material info was saved".

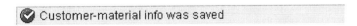

Chapter 6: How to get Overview of Material Stock

We can get stock overview of a particular material across various organization levels by T-Code – MMBE.

Step 1)

Enter T-Code in Command bar MMBE.

Enter Material No .

Select display level for which we want to see stock overview. Click on ⊕ execute Button .

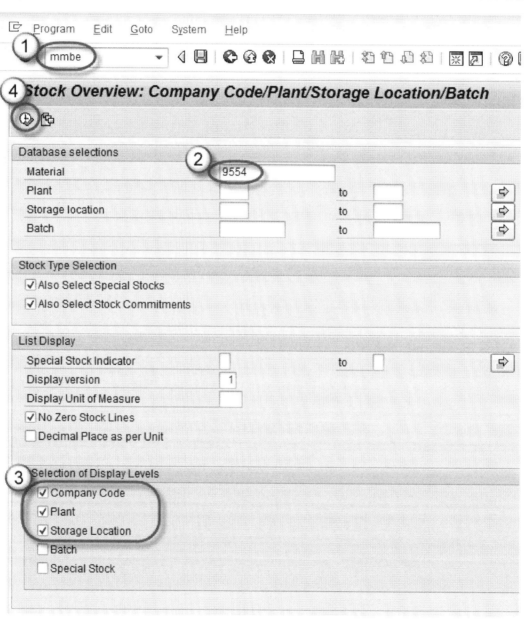

Step 2)
Output will be displayed as below-

1. Stock overview for material 9554 is displayed.

2. Stock at Company /Plant / storage location is displayed. By double clicking each level we can see stock overview at that level.

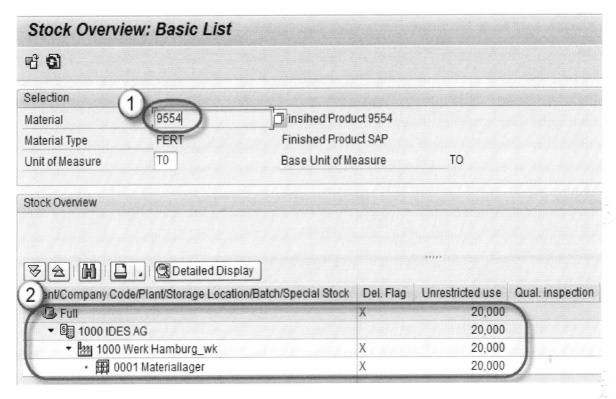

e.g. If we double - click on company level ,then we get detail at company level as below-

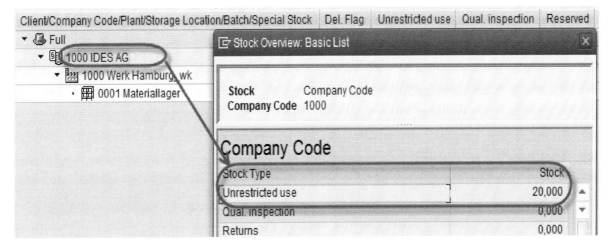

Similarly we can get get stock overview at plant / storage location after double-click on plant / storage level.

Chapter 7: Create Material Master for Sales View

Purpose: This procedure is used to manually create material master for different view. Here sales view is used -

Step 1)

In T-Code MM01 "Create Material"

1. Enter industry sector and material type.

2. Click on Select View(s) Button. A pop window appears. In pop window, select view for which material to be created and click on check button.

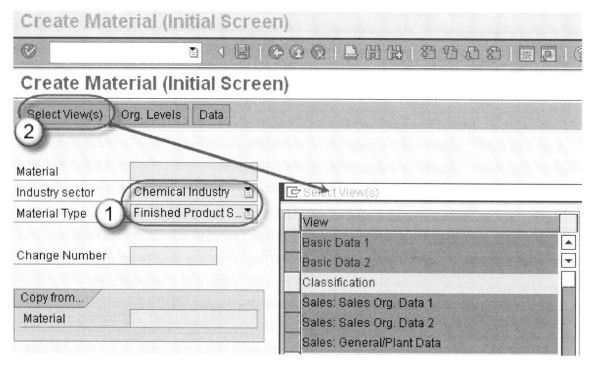

Step 2)

Now a screen appear for all view(w) in Tab screen.

1. Select Basic Data1 tab.

2. Enter material description.

3. Enter Base Unite of Measure.

4. Enter material group.

5. Enter division.

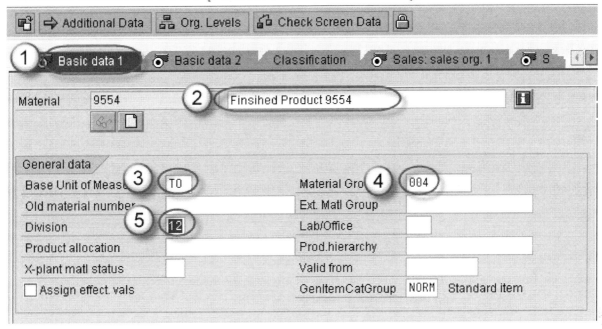

Step 3)

1. Select Sales org 1 Tab screen.

2. Base unit of measure will display.

3. Enter Sales unit.

4. A pop window appear for Conv. factors, enter Conv. factors.

5. Material group is displayed.

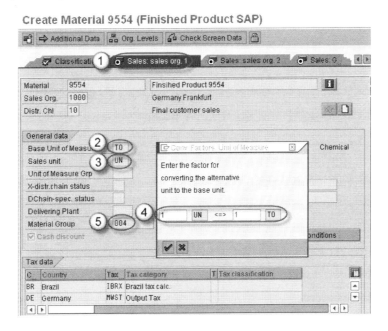

Step 4)

1. Select Sales General / Plant tab screen.

2. Enter Transporter group.

3. Enter Loading group.

Create Material 9554 (Finished Product SAP)

| 🔲 | ➡ Additional Data | 🔠 Org. Levels | 🔠 Check Screen Data | 🔒 |

Sales: sales org. 1 | Sales: sales org. 2 | Sales: General/Plant ① | Forei... | ◀ ▶ ▦

| Material | 9554 | Finsihed Product 9554 | ℹ | ▲ ▼ |
| Plant | 1000 | Werk Hamburg_wk | | |

General data

Base Unit of Measure	TO	Tonnes	Replacement part	
Gross Weight		KG	Qual.f...	
Net Weight			Materi...	
Availability check	01	Daily requirements	App	
☐ Batch management				

Loading Group (1) 16 Entries four...

Restrictions

Shipping ② (times in days)

Trans. Grp	0003		LoadingGrp ③ ☑	LGrp	Description
Setup time		Proc. time	Base qty	0001	Crane
				0002	Forklift
				0003	Manual

Step 5)

click on tab list Icon.

Plant data / stor. 2 | Warehouse Mgmt 1 | Warehouse Mgmt 2 | Quality m... | ◀ 🔲

a list of all tab appear ,select costing tab2 from list.

1. Enter valuation class for material by selection view.

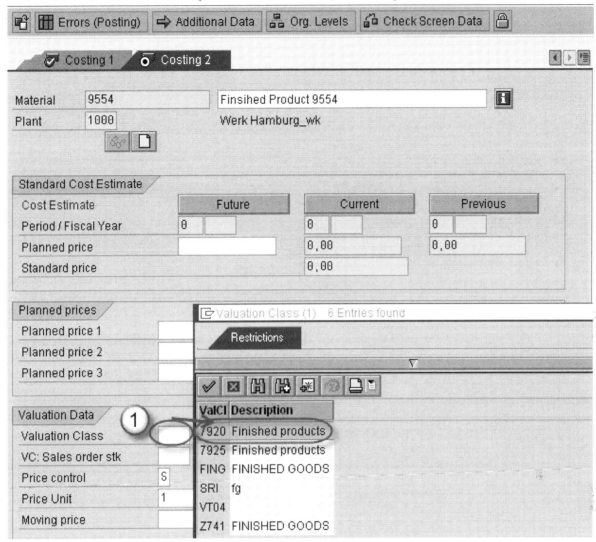

Step 6)

Click on save button. A message "Material 9554 Created".

Chapter 8: Overview of Sales Activities

Normally all Sales activities (leaving out the activities undertaken by Marketing function) can be broadly categorized into pre sales and post sales activities. Pre Sales activity is a process which happen before product is sold to customer.

Pre Sales Documents

They are of 2 types 1) Inquiries and 2) Quotation:

Inquiries : Inquiry documents are customer request for information about product.(e.g. Is product is available, product cost,delivery date etc). T-code for Inquiries is -

- VA11 - Create Inquiry

- VA12 - Change Inquiry

- VA13- Display Inquiry

Quotes: This is a legally binding document to the customer, for delivering product or service to customer T-code for Quotes is -

- VA21 - Create Quotation

- VA22 - Change Quotation

- VA23- Display Quotation

Pre Sales Support

It defines tracking of customer contacts by sales visits, phone calls, letters and direct mailings.

- Customer Tracking : Sales personnel track customer.

- Mailing Campaigns: Sales personnel or company arrange a mailing campaigns to reach customers.

- Customer telephone Queries: Sales support personnel answer Customer queries.

Post Sales activities

These activities include Farming, Relationship Management and Support.

Chapter 9: How to Create Inquiry

Background:

An inquiry document is an internal document .It records the information about the request from prospective customer to be circulated in the company and is not a legal document.

The information captured is mainly the materials and the quantity.More details could be added to the document which is optional. The big advantage of creating inquiry is to reduce any business overhead needed for completing the reply to the customer.

T-code for creating Inquiry is - VA11.

Step 1)

1. Enter T-code VA11 in the command bar field.

2. Select Inquiry Type from help. In screenshot , "IN" is selected for Inquiry.

3. Enter Sales organization / Distribution channel / Division / Sales office / Sales Group.

4. Select Sales Icon

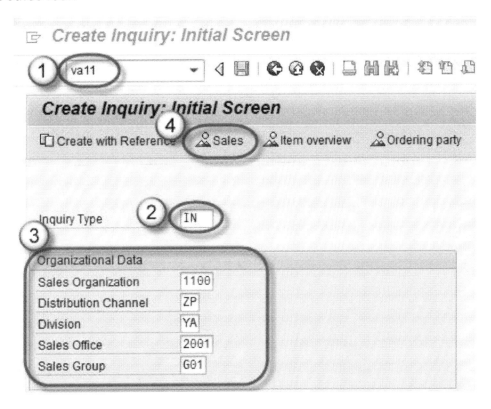

Step 2)

1. Enter Sold-To Party / Ship-To Party (This is Partner Function).

2. Enter Material Code and Quantity .

3. Click on Save 💾 Button.

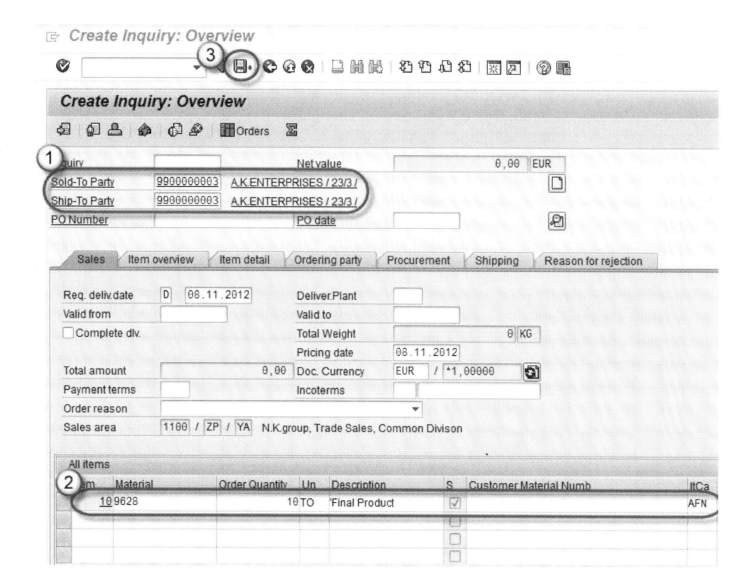

Step 3)

A Message " Inquiry 10000015 has been saved" displayed.

✓ Inquiry 10000015 has been saved

Chapter 10: How to Create Quotation

Quotation:

It's a sales document ,which informs the customer, that company will deliver a specific quantity of product at a specific time and at a specific price.

Quotation can be created after receipt of inquiry from customer or without inquiry.When quotation is created post receipt of inquiry from customer , two methods can be followed -

1. Create quotation with reference to inquiry.

2. Create quotation without reference to inquiry .

The following demonstration creates quotation with reference to inquiry. T-code for create
Quotation : VA21

Step 1)

    1. Enter T-code VA21 in Command field.

    2. Enter quotation type.

    3. Enter Sales Organization / Distribution channel / Division in organizational block.

    4. Select Create with references button .

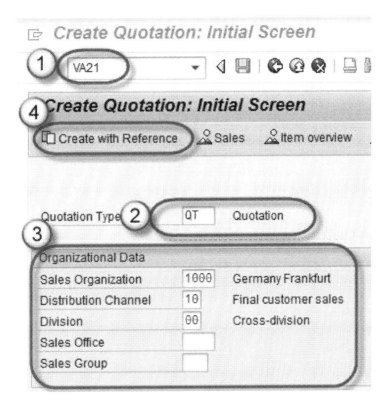

Step 2)

    1. Enter Inquiry Number .

    2. Click on copy button.

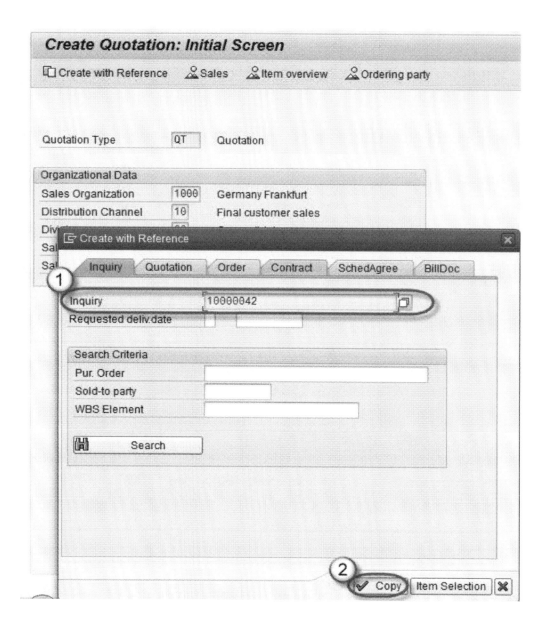

Step3)

1. Enter Ship-To Party.

2. Enter Po Number, if any.

3. Enter Valid from and Valid to date (this is a date until which this quotation will be valid.)

4. Enter Quantity of material.

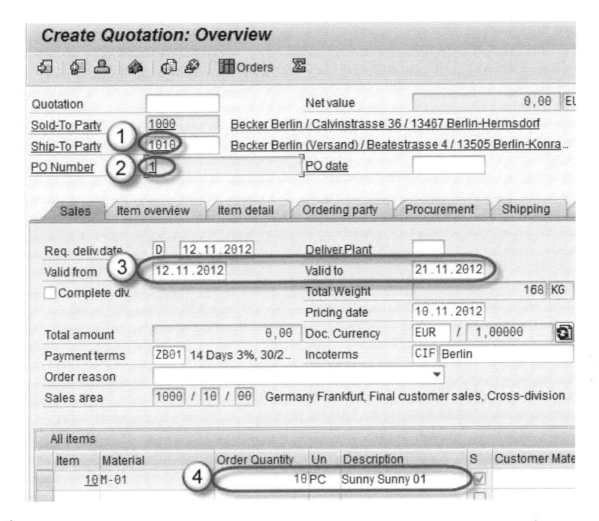

Step 4)

Click on save ⊟ button .

A message "Quotation 20000076 has been saved " will be displayed.

☑ Quotation 20000076 has been saved

Chapter 11: How To Create Sales Order

Background:

A 'Sales Order' is a contract between a Customer and a Sales organization for supply of specified goods and/services over a specified time period. All relevant information from Customer master record and Material master record is copied to the sales order. The sales order may be created with reference to a 'preceding document' such as an inquiry /quotation. In such case, all the initial data from the preceding document is copied to the sales order. T-code -VA01.

Step 1)

1. Enter T-code VA01 in command field.

2. Enter order type OR for Standard order.

3. Enter Sales organization / Distribution Channel / Division in Organizational Data block.

4. Click on create with reference button,for create sales order from Inquiry / Quotation.

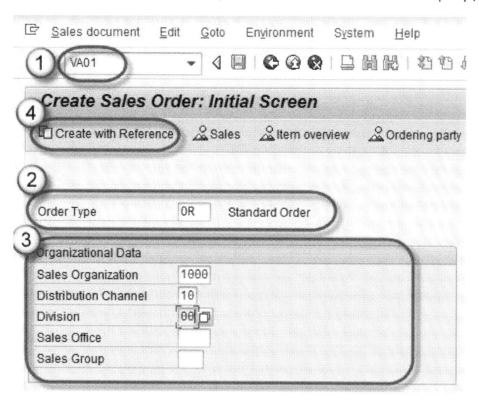

Step 2)

1. Enter quotation number in quotation tab.

2. Select copy button.

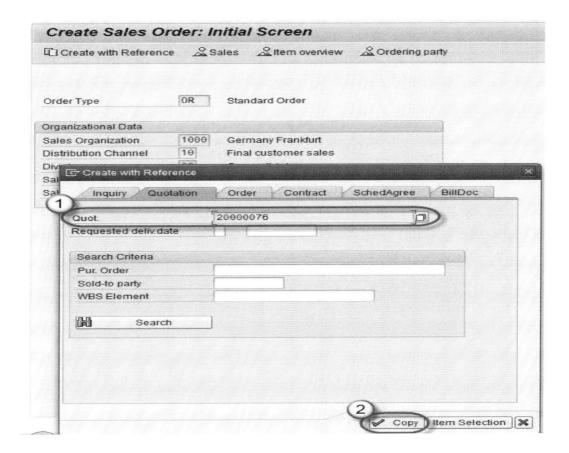

Step 3)

1. Enter Ship-To-Party / PO number / PO date.

2. Enter Req. delivery date.

3. We can change order quantity.

4. Click on save button.

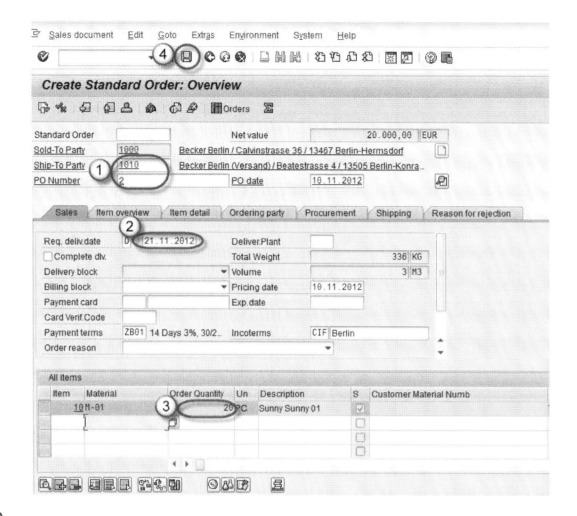

Step 4)

A Message "Standard Order 2000958 has been saved " is displayed.

☑ Standard Order 2000958 has been saved

Chapter 12: How To Create Debit Memo

Background:

Debit Memo Request is a sales document used in sales document processing to request a debit memo for a customer.

Example scenario, a debit memo would be created when price calculated is low due to wrong rates selected.

A debit memo can be blocked ,so that it can be checked & after approval of debit memo,we can process debit memo.

Step 1)

1. Enter T-code VA01 in Command field.

2. Enter in Order Type Debit Memo Request.

3. Enter Sales Organization / Distribution Channel / Division in sales organization tab.

4. Click on Create With References Button.

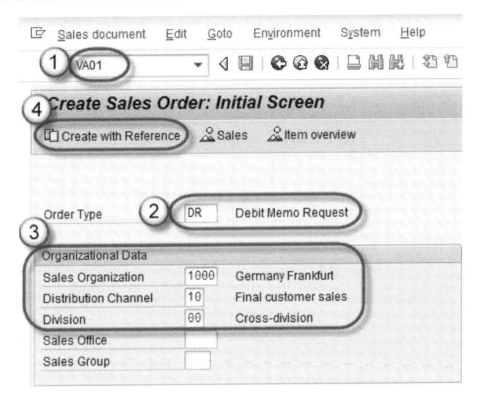

Step 2)

1. Enter Sales Order no for references to create demo memo request in order tab of pop up window.

2. Click on Copy Button.

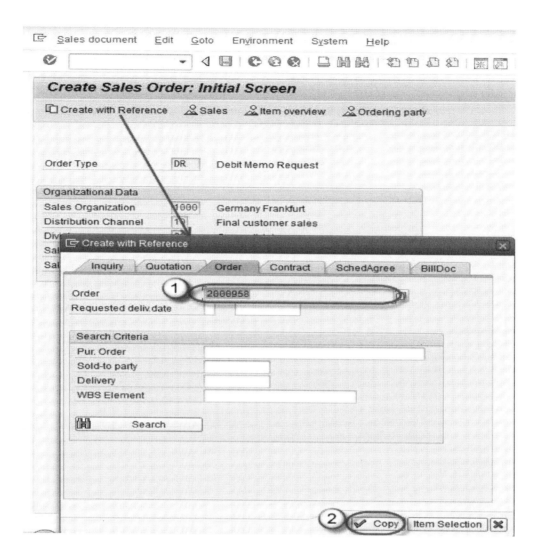

Step 3)

1. Enter Purchase order no.

2. Enter Billing Block(Reason for debit memo) .

3. Enter Pricing Date(*Pricing date* is the date in which the condition records are accessed).

4. Enter Billing Date.

5. Enter Target quantity(quantity for which we creating debit memo).

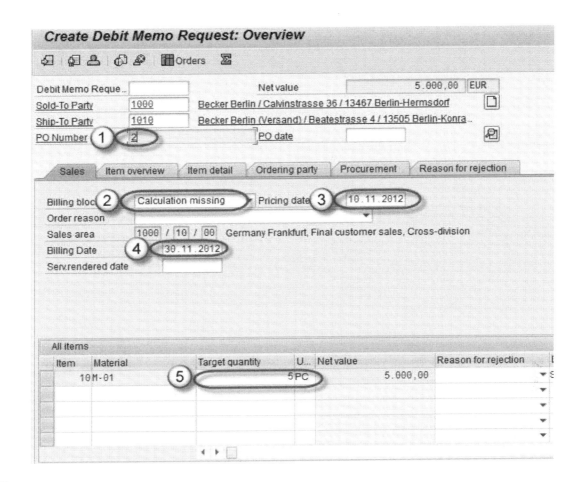

Step 4)

Click on save  button.

A message "Debit Memo Request 700000 has been saved" is displayed.

Chapter 13: How To Create Credit Memo

What is Credit Memo?

It's a sales document used in complaint processing to request credit to customer.Below are some situation for issue credit memo -

- The Price calculated for customer is not correct,e.g. discount is not included in sales document for customer.

- Quantity is not correct in sales document.

Step 1)

1. Enter T-code VA01 in command field.

2. Enter order type field value as credit memo request .

3. Enter Sales Organization / Distribution Channel / Division in Organizational Data.

4. Click on Create with References Button.

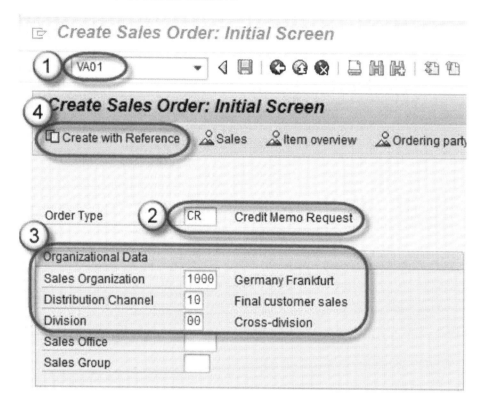

Step 2)

1. Enter order no in Order tab of Pop Up.

2. Click on Copy Button.

Step 3)

1. Enter Billing Block / Pricing Date / Order Reason and Billing Date in sales tab.

2. Enter Material and Target Quantity for which we want to create Credit Memo.

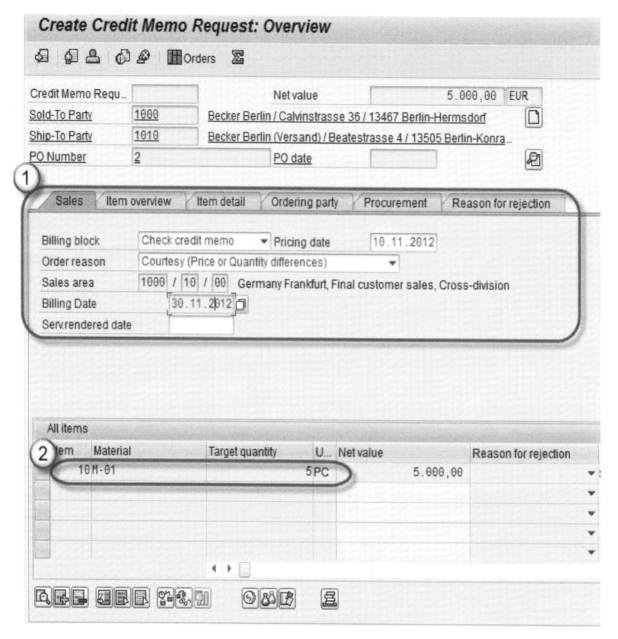

Step 4)

Click on Save ![save] Button .

A message will be displayed " Credit Memo Request 60000189 has been saved'.

☑ Credit Memo Request 60000189 has been saved

Chapter 14: How To Create Sales Document Type

Sales Document Types.

Sales Documents Types is a 2 character indicator, by which system process different documents in different way.SAP provides many standard sales document type. Sales documents types are used in-

- Pre - sales activities (inquiry /quotation).

- Sales Order.

- Sales Contract.

- Customer Complaint.

In Sales order there are three levels –

1. Header level data

2. Item level data

3. Schedule level data

In SAP several standard sales documents types are available.We can create custom sales document type by T-code-VOV8.

Create Internal No. Range for sales document type.

VN01 is T- code for creation for Internal No. range. We will use this internal no. in step-3.

1. Enter T-code VN01 in command field in a new sap session.

2. Click on Create button for interval .

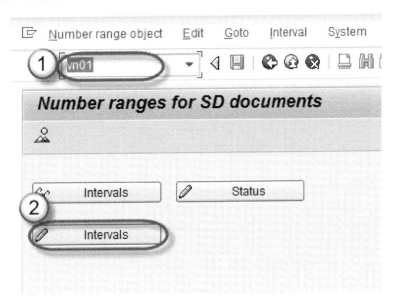

1. Click on +Interval Button to create new interval range.

2. Enter From number / To number / current number / leave blank Ext which stands for External Number Range.

3. Click on save button.

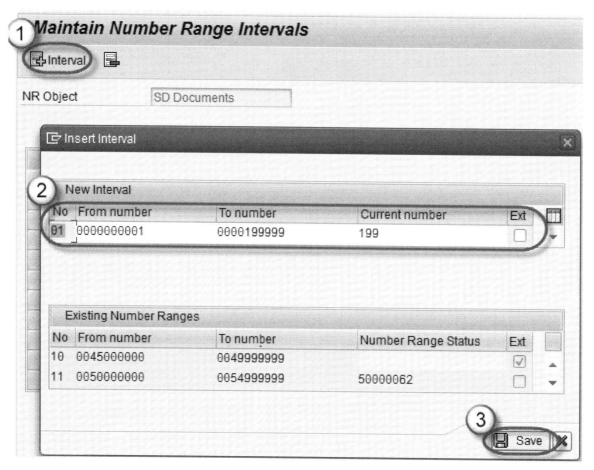

A Message "The changes were saved" is displayed.

Step 1)

1. T-code for sales documents type is VOV8.

2. Sales document types list.

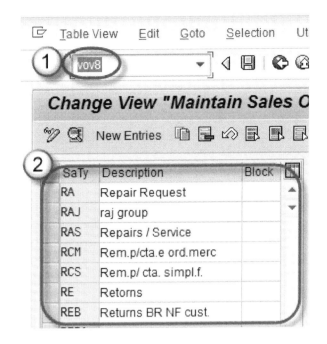

Step 2)

To Create new Sales document type click on New Entries

- Enter sales document type .

- Enter sales document categ from possible entries list.

This screen have multiple section as above-

1. Number System

2. General Control

3. Transaction Flow

4. Scheduling Agreement

5. Shipping

6. Billing

7. Requested Delivery Date

8. Contract

9. Availability Check

Sales Document Type	ZSA0	Sales Order		
SD document categ.	C		Sales document block	
① Indicator				

Number systems

No.range int.assgt.	01		Item no.increment	10
② No. range ext. assg.	02		Sub-item increment	1

General control

Reference mandatory			Material entry type	
Check division			☑ Item division	
Probability	0		☑ Read info record	
Check credit limit	D		Check purch.order no	
Credit group	01		☐ Enter PO number	
③ Output application	V1		Commitment date	

Transaction flow

Screen sequence grp.	AU	Sales Order	Display Range	UALL
Incompl. proced.			FCode for overv.scr.	UER1
Transaction group	0	Sales order	Quotation messages	B
Doc. pric. procedure	A		Outline agrmt mess.	B
Status profile			Message: Mast.contr.	
Alt.sales doc. type1			ProdAttr.messages	
Alt.sales doc. type2			☐ Incomplet.messages	
④ Variant				

Scheduling Agreement

Corr.delivery type			Delivery block	
Usage				
⑤ MRP for DlvSchType				

Shipping

Delivery type	LF	Delivery	Immediate delivery	
Delivery block				
Shipping conditions				
⑥ ShipCostInfoProfile	STANDARD	Standard freight information		

Billing

Dlv-rel.billing type			CndType line items	
Order-rel.bill.type			Billing plan type	
Intercomp.bill.type			Paymt guarant. proc.	
Billing block			Paymt card plan type	
⑦			Checking group	

Requested delivery date/pricing date/purchase order date

Lead time in days			☐ Propose deliv.date	
Date type			☐ Propose PO date	
Prop.f.pricing date				
⑧ Prop.valid-from date				

Contract

PricProcCondHeadr			Contract data allwd.	
PricProcCondItem			FollUpActivityType	
Contract profile			Subseq.order type	
Billing request			Check partner auth.	
⑨ Group Ref. Procedure			☐ Update low.lev.cont.	

Availability check

Business transaction		

We will enter data in Number System / General control / Transaction flow / Shipping Section.

Step 3) Number System

There are two method for define no. range for Sales Document.

- Internal Assignment - This assignment works internally and number for sales document generate automatically.

- External Assignment - This assignment works externally. e.g. in below picture number start from 02.

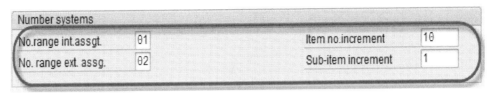

Step 4) General Control

- Enter value in Check credit limit / Credit group / Output application field from possible value list/ check Item Division / Read info record.

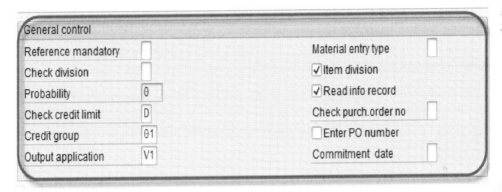

Step 5) Transaction Flow

- Enter value in screen sequence grp. / transaction group / document pricing procedure.

- Enter value in field Display range / Fcode / quotation msg. / Outline agreement msg.

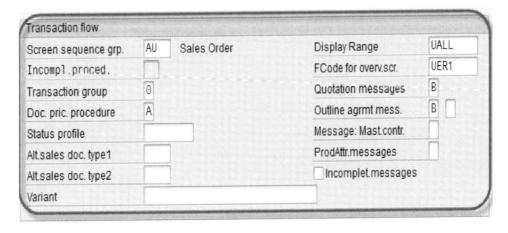

Step 6)

- Enter value in delivery type filed from possible list entry.

- Enter ship cost info profile from possible list entry.

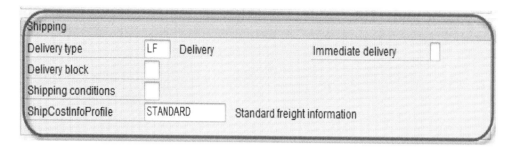

Step 7)

Click on Save 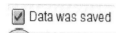 Button.

A Message "Data was saved".

☑ Data was saved

Chapter 15: All about Sales Document (header / item / schedule)

Sales Order is a contract between a customer and sales organization for supplying goods or service to customer within a agreed time period. Data on the sales order screen is derived from Customer Master Table and Material Master Table for a particular sales area.The sales area that accepts the inquiry is responsible for completing the contract. T-code for sales order is -

1. VA01- Create sales order.

2. VA02-Change sales order.

3. VA03-Display sales order.

To create sales order we need data at four levels-

1.Organization data : Organization data is first screen of sales document which contains fields like Sales organization,distribution channel,division,Sales Office ,Sales Group etc.

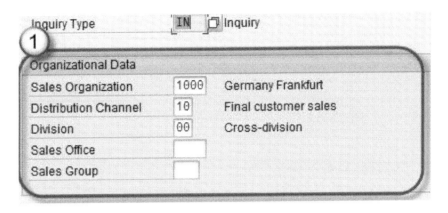

2.Header data : Sales order header contain many tab(sales,shipping,billing etc.). Header essentially contains information mostly from the Customer Master in the Transaction. We can click on header ![button] button for sales header screen display.

Inquiry	10000023	Net value	31.000,00	EUR
Sold-To Party	T-S62A16	Etelko Textilien / Kirchstr. 53 / 55124 Mainz		
Ship-To Party	T-S62A16	Etelko Textilien / Kirchstr. 53 / 55124 Mainz		
PO Number	123456789	PO date		

Sales Header screen is displayed as below -

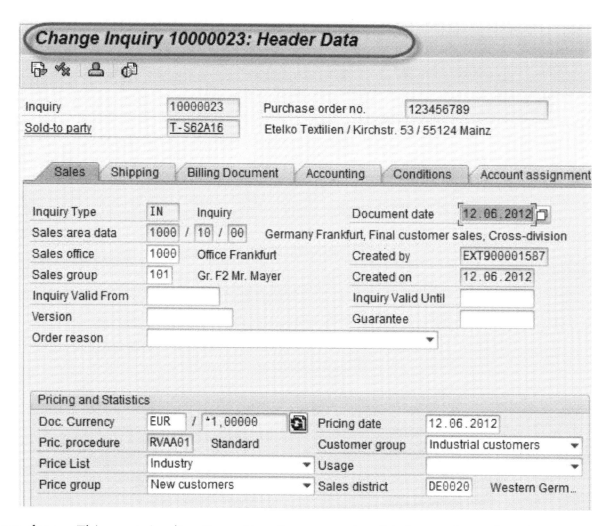

3. Item data : This contains line item .Line item contain all information related to customer / material / quantity .

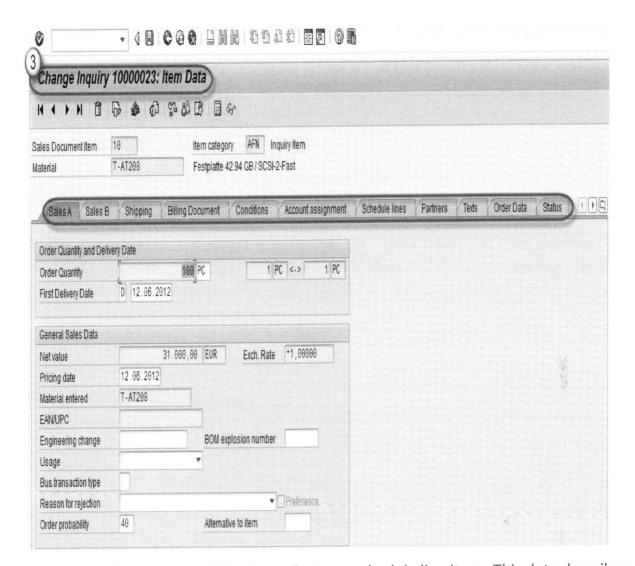

4 . Schedule line data : For each line item their are schedule line items.This data describes quantity and date. Select item lines for item data and click on schedule line 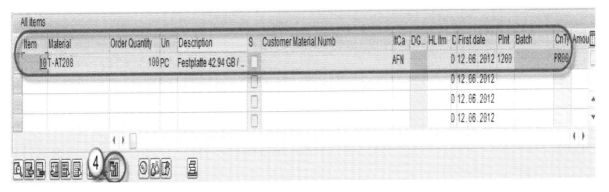 buttons.

Click on schedule line button AGAIN -

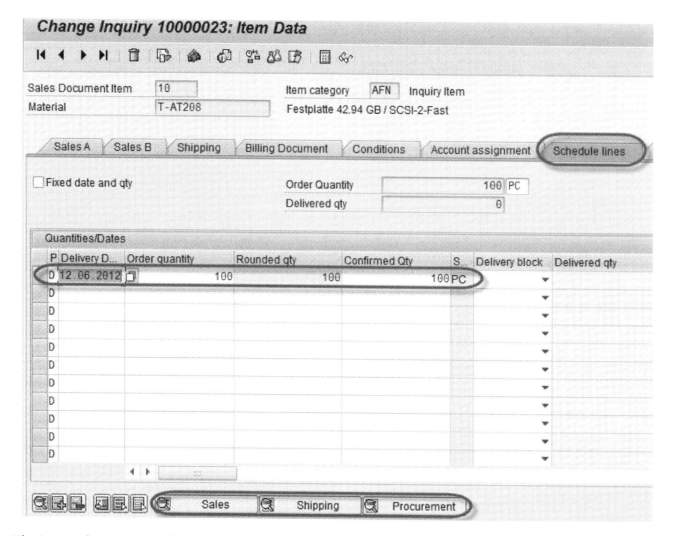

Their are three views for schedule line -

- Sales : Delivery date / time / quantity.

- Shipping: it contains shipping / delivery / route etc details.

- Procurement : It contains plant / item / quantity details.

Chapter 16: Text determination for sales document header / item

Text can be used to exchange the information via documents with a partner and end users. Text can be created for objects like customer master, sales document header and item, billing document header and item as well as condition records. Text can be customer text, sales text, item note, packing note etc. SAP uses condition technique to determine text..

Material master contains text about the material, but this text is not sufficient to create sales order for this material by sales person. So system ensures text about a sales document item.

There are a number of texts like purchase order text, Sales order text, item note, packing note. The texts is picked from corresponding master data (Material master etc.) or entered manually in screen.

Material sales text comes from the master data (sales view of material master) to the line item in the sales order. For this system need to configured accordingly. The process of creating and configuring new texts for flow in the transaction and to define when and where texts will be called is know as "**Text Determination**".

Text determination for sales document header.

Step 1)

1. Enter T-code VOTXN in the command field.

2. Select Sales document header radio button.

3. Click on change button.

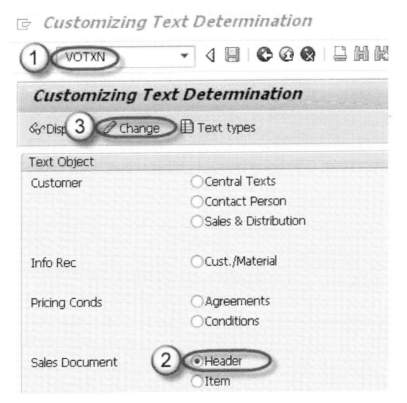

Step 2)

1. Select Text procedure and click on new entries button.

2. Enter Text procedure and description.

3. Click on save button.

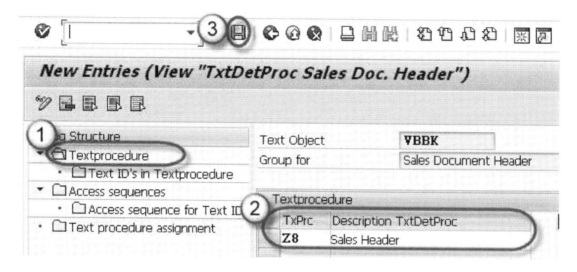

Step 3)

1. Select Text procedure assignment node.

2. Assign text procedure to sales document type.

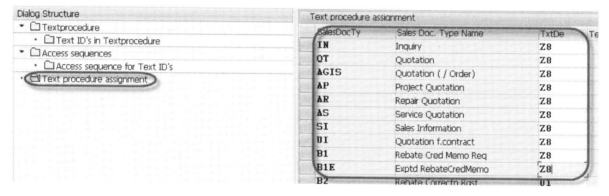

Step 4) Click on save button.

Text determination for sales document Item.

Step 1)

1. Enter T-code VOTXN in command field.

2. Select Sales document item radio button.

3. Click on change button.

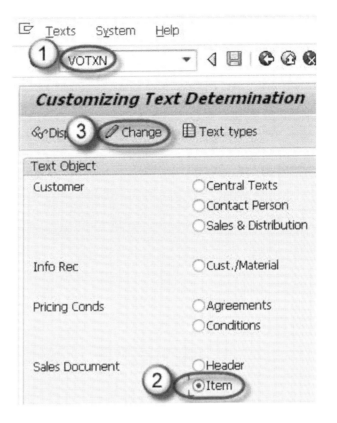

Step 2)

1. Select text procedure node.

2. Click on New Entries button.

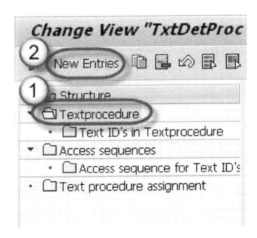

Step 3)

1. Select text procedure button.

2. Enter Text procedure and description.

3. Click on save button.

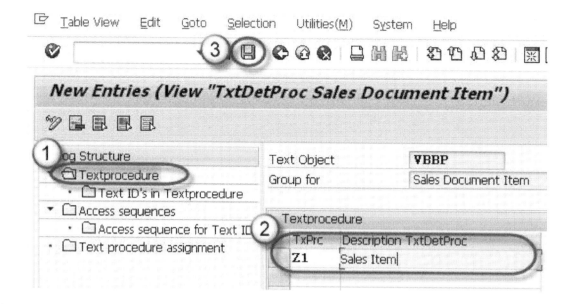

Step 4)

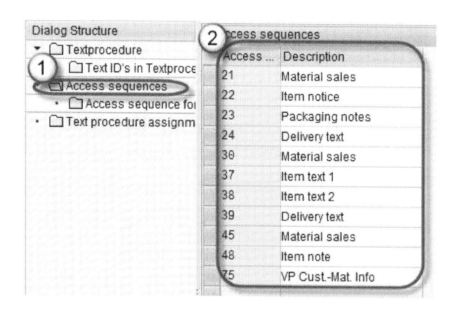

Step 5)

1. Select Text ID's in text procedure node.

2. Assign Sequence no. to Text ID.

3. Click on save button.

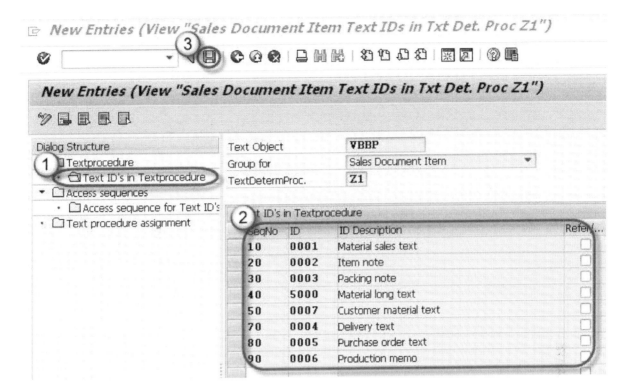

Step 6)

1. Select Text procedure assignment.

2. Assign Text Procedure to item category.

3. Click on save button.

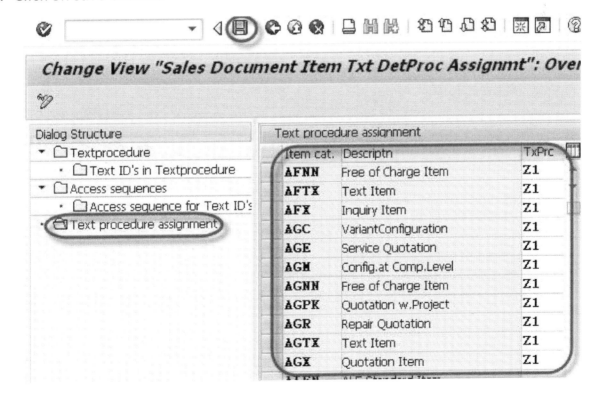

Chapter 17: What is Schedule Line Category and how to define it

What is Schedule Line Category?

SAP System only copies those items of sales document ,which have schedule line .Schedule lines contain all the delivery related information such as: delivery dates and quantities as well as information about the requirements transfer and inventory management.

Schedule line category has two alphanumeric key.

1) First character of key uses -

Char	Uses
A	Inquiry
B	Quotation
C	Sales order
D	Returns

2)Second character of key uses -

Char	Uses
T	no inventory management, e.g. services
X	no inventory management with goods issue
N	no planning
P	MRP

Char	Uses
V	consumption-based planning

Schedule Line category in different sales document. Inquiry:

- No availability check .

- Not relevant for delivery.

- Schedule line is for information purpose.

Quotation:

- Schedule line is not relevant for delivery.

- No Movement type(Movement type describes type of material movement).

Order :

- Schedule line is relevant for delivery.

- Movement type is 601.

Return:

- Schedule line is relevant for delivery.

- Movement type is 651.

Define schedule line category

We can define our Schedule line category by three ways -

1. Copy an exiting Schedule line category and change according our requirements.

2. Change an exiting Schedule line category.

3. Create a new Schedule line category.

Step 1)

1. Enter T-code VOV6 in command field.

2. List of exiting schedule line category displayed.

3. To Create New Schedule line category,click on new entries 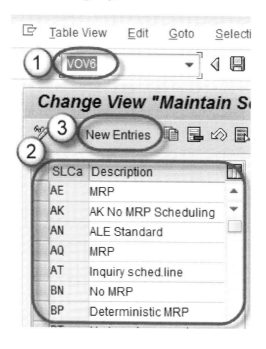 New Entries button.

Step 2)

1. Enter Schedule line item category and it's description.

2. Enter Movement type(It is used to describe the type of material movement that need to be performed). e.g receipts, issues, transfers, reversal.

3. Enter Order Type / item category / Acct. Assgt cat.

4. Check on Item rel.f.dlv/Preq.del.sched.

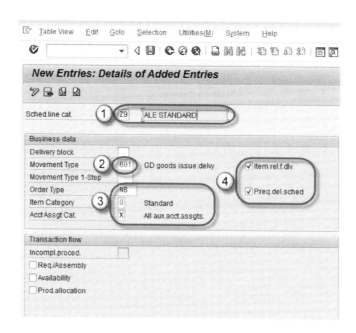

Step 3) Click on Save 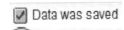 Button. A Message as "Data Was Saved " displayed.

Chapter 18: How to create Item Proposal

What is Item Proposal?

Item proposal is the list of materials and order quantities that can be copied into the sales order .Item proposal is same as product proposal and SAP uses the two terms interchangeably."MS" is a standard document type for Product Proposal.A customized document type can be created for item proposal by T-code –VOV8.

VA51 is T-code for creating Item Proposal.This T-code gives a number upon saving,which is linked to the customer data in sales view.

Step 1)

1. Enter T-code VA51 in the command field.

2. Enter Item proposal type .

3. Enter Sales organization / Distribution Channel / Division.

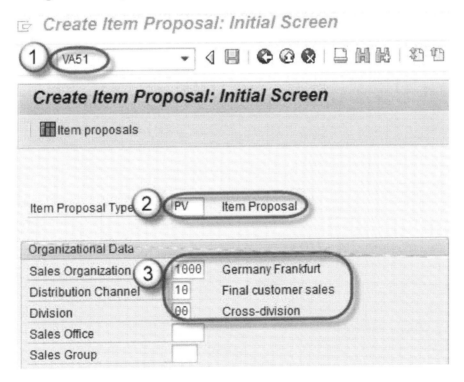

Step 2)

1. Enter Proposal number / description / Valid from date / Valid To date.

2. Enter Material No./ Quantity.

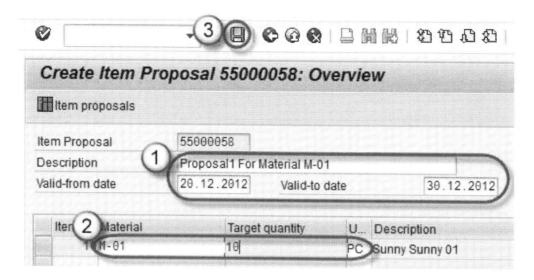

Step 3)

1. Click on Save 🖫 Button.

2. A message "Item Proposal 50000071 has been saved".

☑ Item Proposal 55000058 has been saved

Chapter 19: All About Material Exclusion & Inclusion (Listing)

What is Exclusion List?

Material exclusion / listing is a provision to restrict a customer's buying choices. For example, if certain materials are defined in "**Exclusion List**" of a specific customer, then, the customer can not buy material from "Exclusion List".

Example – A company produce 10 materials and company want to sell only 6 material to customer ABC then company create a list of these 6 material as "Listing List "(products that can be ordered) and remaining 4 material may be in "Exclusion List". In this scenario Customer can buy only 6 material from "**Listing List**".

Material exclusion / listing is controlled by **condition technique**. System check for material in "Exclusion List" first and later "Listing List". T-code- 1. VB01 to create, 2. VB02 to change, 3. VB03 to display.

Material Exclusion

Step 1)

1. Enter T-code VB01 in command bar.

2. Click on exclusion type field.

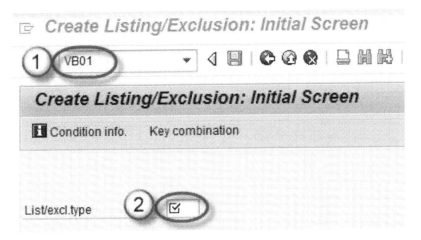

Select B001 in popup window as shown below

Step 2)

1. Enter Customer code and validity period.

2. Enter material code for exclusion list.

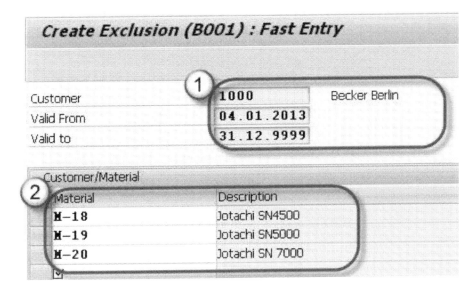

Step 3)

Click on save button . A message "Condition records saved" will be displayed.

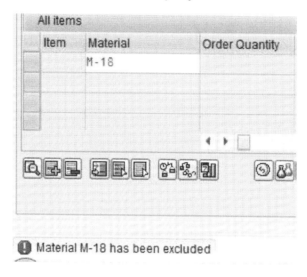

When a user create sales order by t-code VA01 ,for material M-18 ,for customer # 1000 , a message "Material M-18 has been excluded" displayed.

Material Listing

Step 1)

1. Enter T-code VB01 in command field.

2. Select List type .

Select A001 in pop up as displayed below-

Step 2)

1. Enter Customer code ,Valid From / to date .

2. Enter all material code which customer # 1000 can purchase.

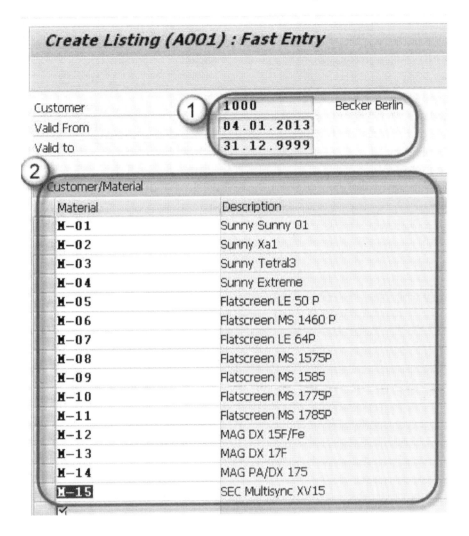

Step 3)

Save the record.

A message "Condition records saved" will be displayed.

☑ Condition records saved

Chapter 20: How to Determine Shipping Point

What is Shipping Point?

Shipping Point is an independent organizational entity, wherein goods issuance and delivery processing takes place. A shipping point can be determined for each order item. Shipping point determination depends on the following three factors-

1. Shipping terms and conditions from the customer master record (shipping screen). E.g Company agreed with customer to deliver product as soon as possible.

2. Loading group from the material master (Sales/Plant data screen). E.g Loading group defines that the product is always loaded by crane.

3. Delivering plant (A plant from where the product will be delivered .A shipping point can be assigned to delivering plant and plant can have multiple shipping point).

Step 1)

1. Enter T-code in OVL2 in command field.

2. Click on New Entries Button.

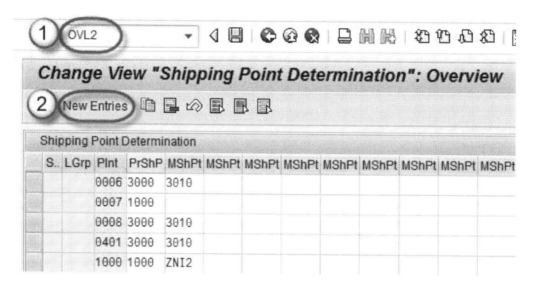

Step 2)

- Enter Shipping condition.

- Enter Loading Group.

- Enter Plant (Plant is place where goods are manufactured or stored).

- Enter proposed shipping point (shipping point is a place within the plant from where company ship the goods to the customer).

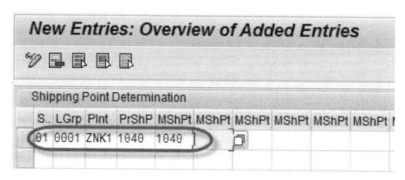

Step 3)

Click on Save 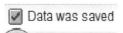 Button .

A message "Data was saved " displayed.

Chapter 21: How to create Picking ,Packing and PGI

What is Picking?

It is necessary to prepare correct quantity and quality of goods as specified in sales order for shipping on schedule as required by the customer. Material picking is done by warehouse management(WM). WM picking is done via transfer order. The transfer order is the basis for the picking list, it is used to withdraw the ordered goods from stock. There are three ways of picking-

1. Pick Delivery individually.

2. Picking can be scheduled to run at per-defined intervals.

3. SAP SD module can be configured to execute picking automatically.

What is Packing?

Packing function is used to exchange product data between suppliers and customers. The packing of product is done by the packing material. These packing materials need to be created in the material master with material type "VERP". Packing can we done in SAP in two ways-

1. Manual Packing

2. Automatic Packing

There are many Steps in packing function like manual packing and auto packing with single level and multilevel packing.

What is Post Good Issue (PGI)?

Post goods issue is the last Step of delivery/shipment processing. Herein, ownership of the goods transfer to the customer and the stock is updated. The carrier in turn transfers the ownership to the final customer once goods are delivered.

Steps for Picking ,Packing and PGI are as below-

1. Create outbound delivery with reference to sales order.

2. Create picking request.

3. Creating Packing.

4. Create PGI.

Step 1) Create Outbound delivery

1. Enter T-code VL01N in command bar.

2. Enter Shipping Point.

3. Enter Selection Date and sales order.

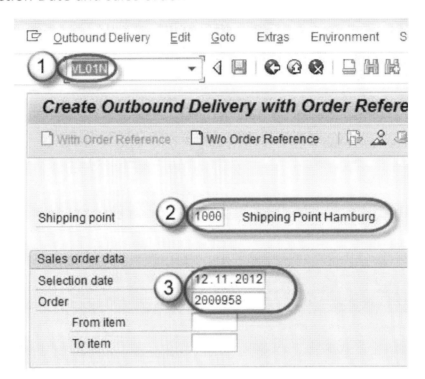

Click on save  button.

A message "Delivery 80016014" has been saved.

Step 2) Creating Picking Request

1. Enter T-code LT03 in command field.

2. Enter warehouse Number / Plant / Delivery and press enter .

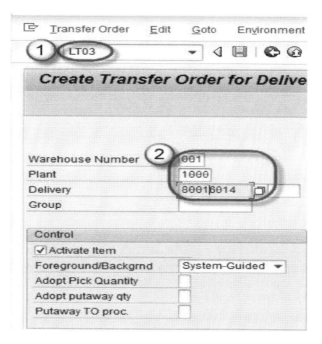

Click on save ⊞ Button.

A Message" Transfer order 0000002638 created" will be displayed.

☑ Transfer order 0000002638 created

Step 3) Create Packing

1. Enter T-code VL02N in command field.

2. Enter outbound delivery no,which was created earlier.

3. Click on Pack button.

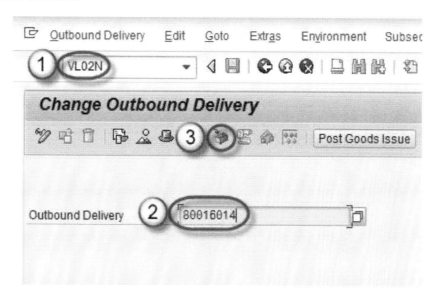

In the next screen,

1. Select Tab "Pack material"

2. Enter packing material detail.

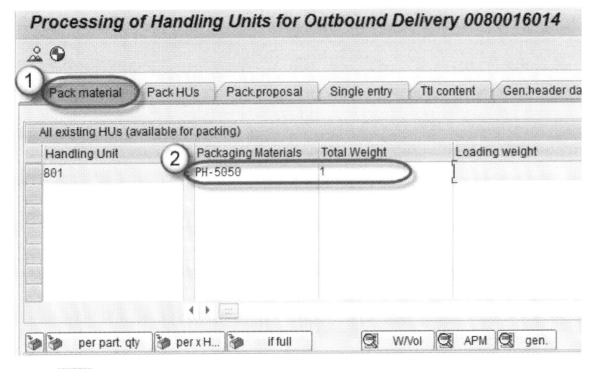

Click on save 🖫 button.

✓ Delivery 80016014 has been saved

Step 4) Post Good Issue (PGI).

By PGI (Post Goods Issue) the owner ship of the material or goods will be changed from company to the customer.

1. Enter T-code VL02N in command field.

2. Enter Outbound Delivery number.

3. Click on Post Goods issue Button.

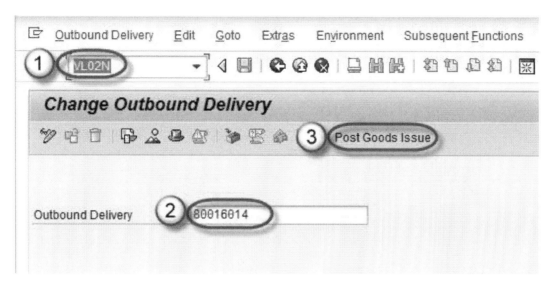

A message "Replenishment dlv. has been saved" is shown. When we do PGI , two documents will be created-

- **Material document (**Regarding stock reduction)

1. Enter T-code MB03 in command field and Enter sales order no in sales order field and execute the report.

2. Material document will be displayed .

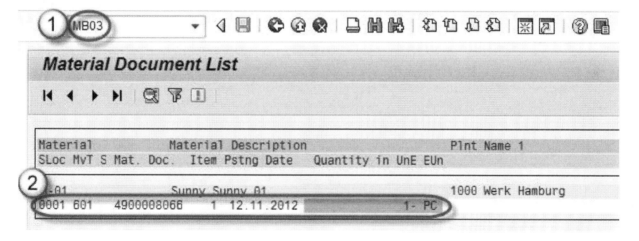

- **Accounting document** (Cost of goods sold will credited and stock value will be debited.)

1. Enter T-Code S_ALR_87014387 in command field.

2. Enter Material code.

3. Click on execute button.

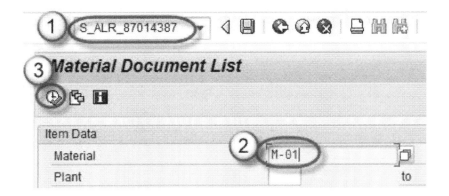

Chapter 22: Returns, Free of Charge Delivery, Sub-sequent Delivery

What is a Return?

Return is where a customer is not satisfied with the product or the deliverable, & businesses need to create a return the good, based on customer return request.

What is Free of Charge Delivery ?

Free of Charge Delivery is where the customer is not charged for shipping. This order type is generally used for sending free sample to customers.

What is Subsequent Delivery?

Subsequent Deliver is when a customer receives lesser number of goods than that ordered, or if the goods have been damaged in the shipment, businesses provide free-of-charge subsequent delivery of goods.

What to do when a customer raises return request ?

Sales Department may take any one of the following actions during the return process.

1. Approve the complaint and create a credit memo.This is done when customer wants refund for the goods. The system creates credit memo to customer with reference to sales order.

2. Approve the complaint, and implement a free of charge subsequent delivery of the disputed goods. This is done when customer want to replace the goods owing to shortfall in delivery or damage in shipment or any other legitimate reasons.

3. Reject the complaint if complaint is not valid. For example, customer makes a complaint on wrong data.

How to Create Return Order

Sales Department can create return order by T-code VA01. Return order can be created with reference to sales order or billing documents.

Step 1)

1. Enter T-code VA01 in command field.

2. Enter Order Type RE(Returns).

3. Enter Sales Area data in Organizational Data Block.

4. Click on Create with Reference Button.

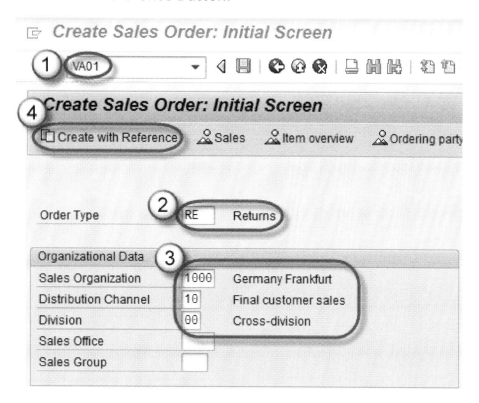

Step 2)

1. Enter Sales order # reference for return order.

2. Click on Copy Button.

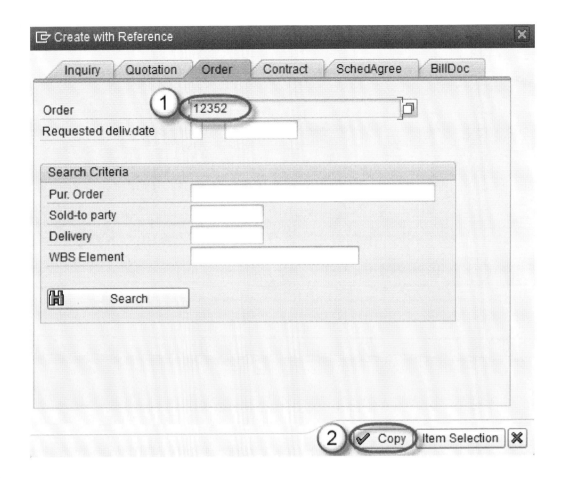

Step 3)

1. Enter PO number.

2. Enter PO date.

3. Enter Order reason .

4. Enter Ordered Quantity.

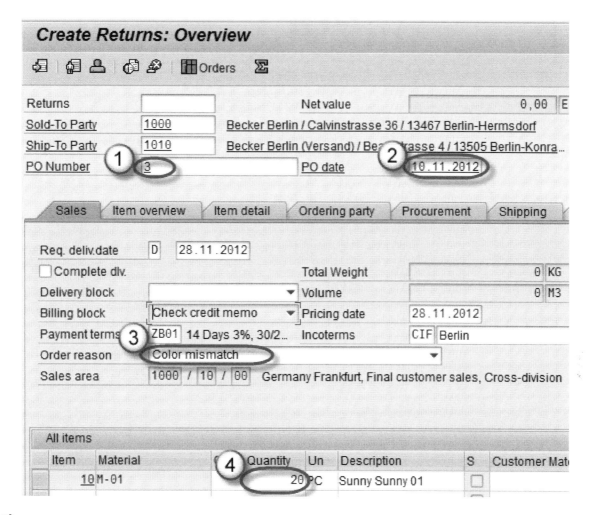

Step 4)

Click on save  button. A Message like "Return 60000295 has been saved" displayed.

☑ Returns 60000195 has been saved

How to create Return Delivery Document

In order to receive returned goods from customer, Sales department creates return order. Based on return order, return delivery document is created. Return delivery document is created using T-code VL01N. Standard return delivery document type is LR. When return delivery document is created,Logistic departments receives the returned product.

Step 1)

1. Enter T-code VL01N in command field.

2. Enter Shipping Point.

3. Enter Delivery Type LR(Return Delivery).

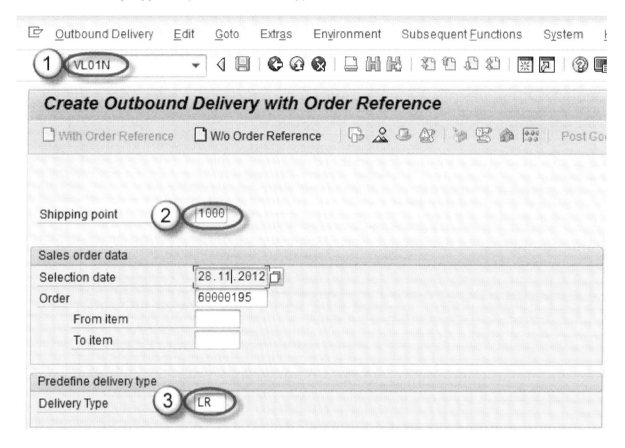

Press Enter Button.

Step 2)

Enter Return Delivery Quantity.

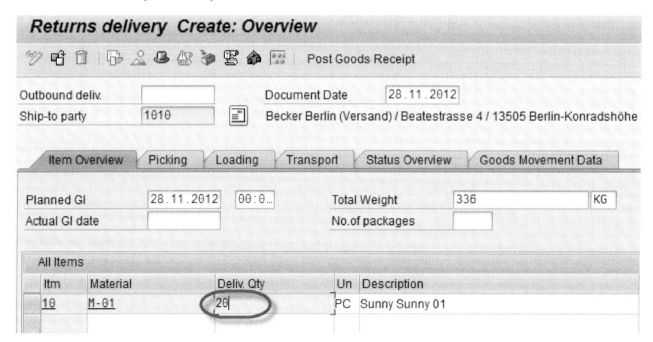

Step 3)

Click on save  button.

A message "Return delivery 840000 has been saved" displayed.

✅ Returns delivery 84000056 has been saved

How to create Free of Charge Delivery

Free of charge delivery process creates a non-billed sales order .E.g. If some product is shipped for free sample to customer, free of charge delivery is carried out.This document is not relevant for billing because the customer is not billed for the free of charge delivery.

Step 1)

1. Enter T-code VA01 in command field.

2. Enter Order type FD(Delivery Free of Charge).

3. Enter Sales area data in Organizational block.

4. Click on Create with References.

Step 2)

1. Enter Sales order no. for references.

2. Click on Copy button.

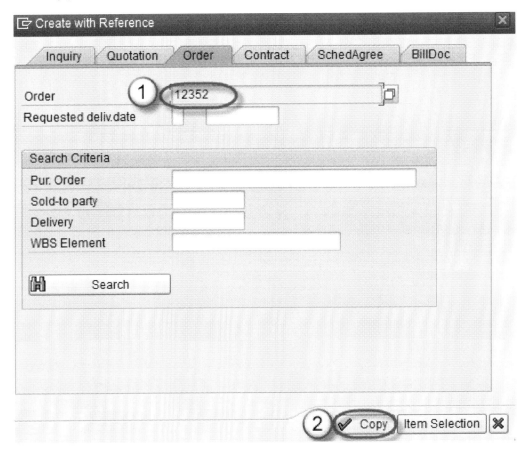

Step 3)

1. Enter Sold-To party / Ship-To Party.

2. Enter Order Reason.

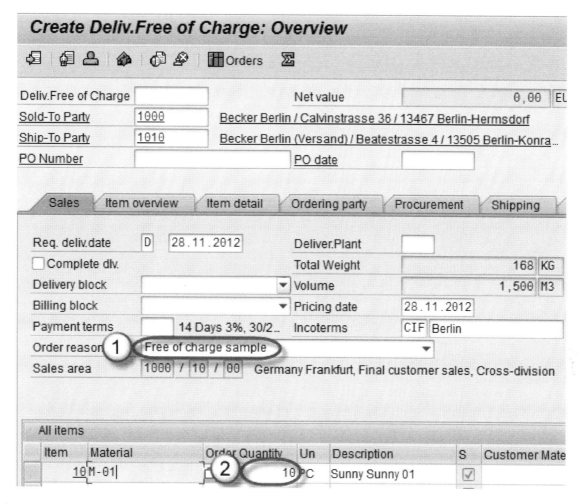

Step 4)

Click on Save  button.

> ☑ Deliv.Free of Charge 12353 has been saved

How to create Subsequent Delivery

Once return process takes place,customer may request

1. Good replacement

2. Refund.

When customer chooses replacement option,then subsequent sales order is created.If customer chooses refund option,then money can be refunded to customer by credit memo.

Step 1)

1. Enter T-code VA01.

2. Enter Order Type SDF .

3. Enter Sales Area data in Organizational Data.

4. Click on Create with References Button.

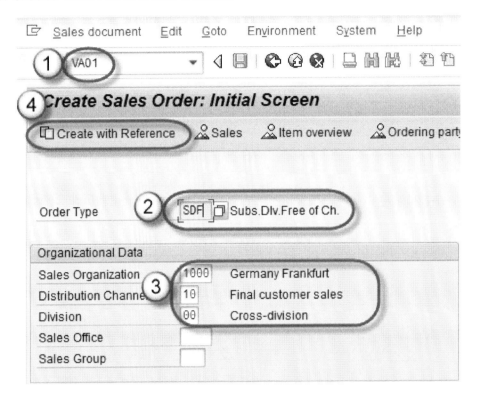

Step 2)

1. Enter Sales Order no. for references.

2. Click on Copy button.

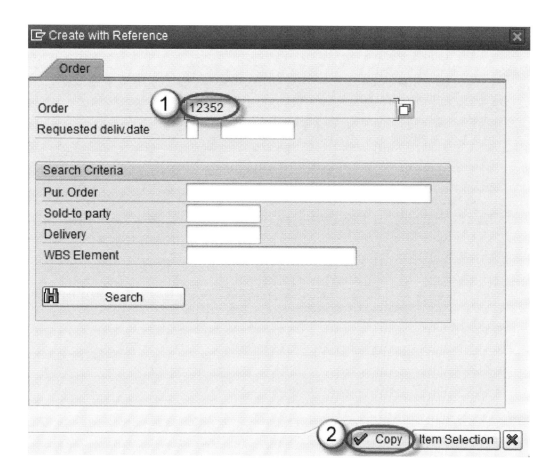

Step 3)

1. Enter Order Reason.

2. Enter Order Quantity for which we create Subsequent Delivery free of charge.

Create Subs.Dlv.Free of Ch.: Overview

Orders

Subs.Dlv.Free of Ch.		Net value	0,00 E
Sold-To Party	1000	Becker Berlin / Calvinstrasse 36 / 13467 Berlin-Hermsdorf
Ship-To Party	1010	Becker Berlin (Versand) / Beatestrasse 4 / 13505 Berlin-Konra...
PO Number		PO date	

| Sales | Item overview | Item detail | Ordering party | Procurement | Shipping |

Req. deliv.date	D	07.12.2012	Deliver.Plant	
☐ Complete dlv.			Total Weight	0 KG
Delivery block		▾	Volume	0 M3
Billing block		▾	Pricing date	28.11.2012
Payment term	①	ZB01 14 Days 3%, 30/2...	Incoterms	CIF Berlin
Order reason		Color mismatch	▾
Sales area		1000 / 10 / 00	Germany Frankfurt, Final customer sales, Cross-division

All items

Item	Material	② Order Quantity	Un	Description	S	Customer Mat
10	M-01	10 PC		Sunny Sunny 01	☐	

Step 4) Click on Save ▯ Button.

A message Subs. Dlv. Free of Ch. 12355 has been saved" displayed.

☑ Subs.Dlv.Free of Ch. 12355 has been saved

Chapter 23: All About Consignment Process

Consignment Process is where product are stored at the customer location but the owner of this product is still company. Customer stores the consignment stock at their own a warehouse. Customer can consume product from warehouse at any time and customer billed for product for actually quantity consumes. In Consignment Stock Processing, there are four main transactions in the SAP System, all of which support separate management of stock:

- Consignment Fill-Up (Stock Fill up at warehouse).

- Consignment Issue (Stock issue from warehouse).

- Consignment Return (Stock return from customer).

- Consignment Pickup (Stock return to manufacture).

Consignment Fill-Up

Consignment Fill-Up is a process, in which company store product at customer sites and still company is the owner of this product. This process is known as consignment fill up (**CF**). Sales order type for consignment filling is – **KB**.

In consignment fill up only order and delivery takes place.

Step 1) Create Consignment Fill Up

1. Enter T-code VA01 in the command field.

2. Enter Order type CF(consignment fill up).

3. Enter sales area in organizational data.

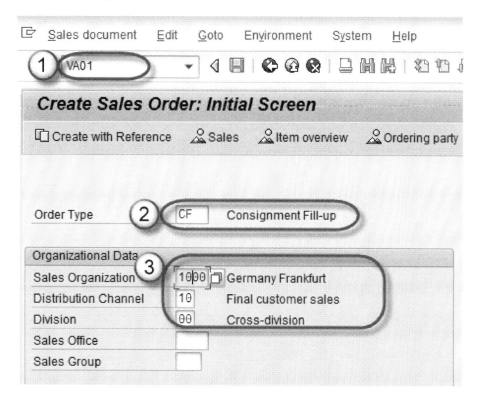

Step 2)

1. Enter PO number.

2. Enter PO Date.

3. Enter Order Quantity.

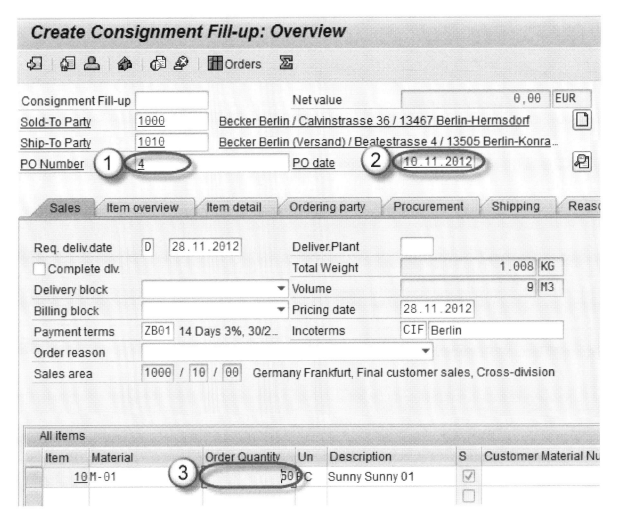

Step 3)

Click on save 🖫 button.

A message as below is displayed.

☑ Consignment Fill-up 12356 has been saved

Consignment Issue

The customer can access product at any time to sell or their use from their warehouse and company will issue invoices for only accessed product, and this invoices known as the consignment issue (**CI**). Sales order type for consignment issue is – **KE.**

In consignment Issue Order, Delivery and Invoices take place.

Step 1)

1. Enter T-code VA01 in command field.

2. Enter order type CI (Consignment issue).

3. Enter Sales area data in Organizational data block.

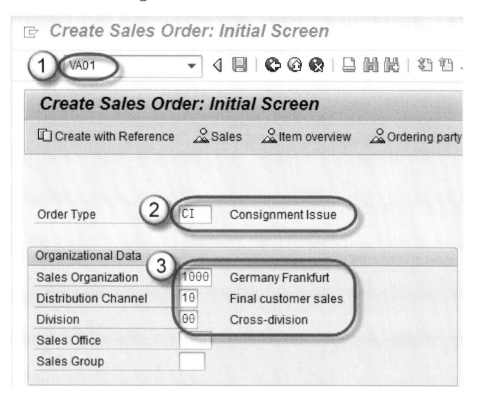

Step 2)

1. Enter Sold-To party / Ship-to Party / PO number.

2. Enter PO Date.

3. Enter Material and ordered quantity.

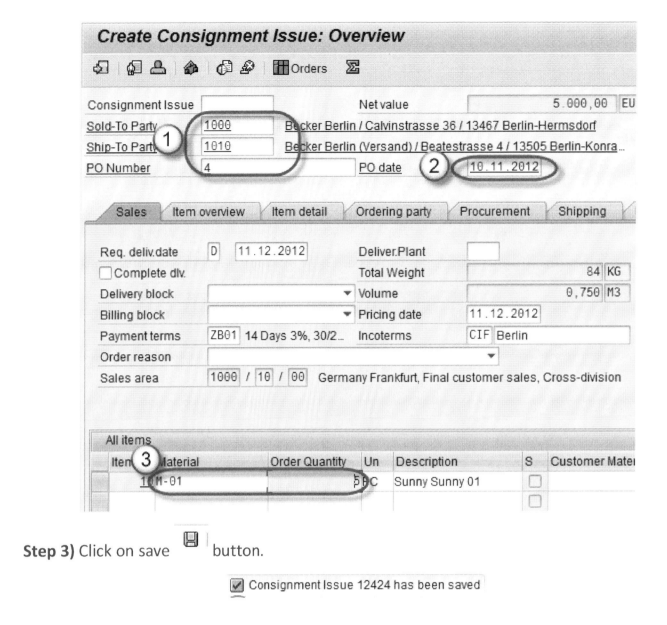

Step 3) Click on save 🖫 button.

☑ Consignment Issue 12424 has been saved

Consignment Return

If customer return product due to damage ,poor quality, expiry, then this process is called consignment return (**CONR**). Consignment return happens after consignment issue. i.e customer can return Consignment product, the product are issued to customer by Consignment issue process. Sales order type for consignment issue is – **KA**.

In consignment Return Order, Delivery, Invoices and Credit for return take place.

Step 1)

1. Enter T-code VA01 in command field.

2. Enter order type CONR(Consignment Returns).

3. Enter Sales area data in Organizational Data block.

Step 2)

1. Enter Sold-to Party / Ship-to party.

2. Enter Order reason.

3. Enter Material and ordered quantity.

Step 3)

Click on save 🖫 button.

> ☑ Consignment Returns 60000197 has been saved

Consignment Pickup

When a customer request to the company ,to take back the product, the company will pack this product from customer sites, this process is known as Consignment Pickup (**CP**). In consignment pickup process , product are not issued to customer and only stored at customer warehouse as consignment stock. Sales order type for consignment issue is – **KR**.

In consignment Pickup Order,Return Delivery takes place.

Step 1)

1. Enter T-code VA01 in command field.

2. Enter Order type CP(Consignment pickup).

3. Enter Sales Area data in Organizational Data block.

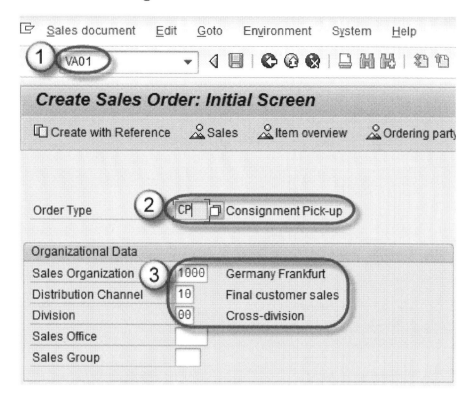

Step 2)

1. Enter Sold-to Party / Ship-to party.

2. Enter Order reason.

3. Enter Material and ordered quantity.

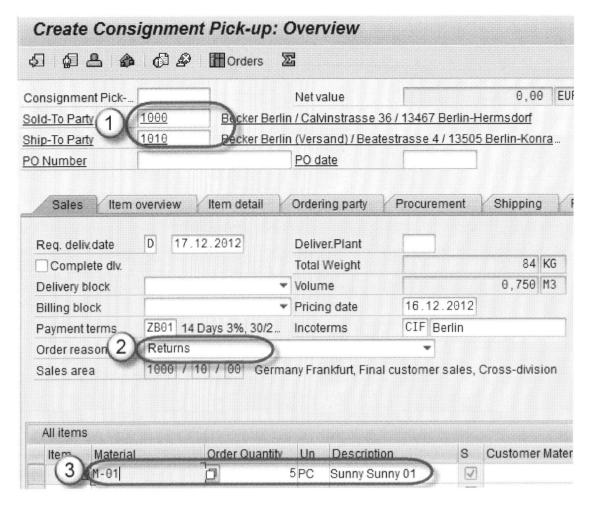

Step 3)

Click on save 💾 button.

Chapter 24: Output proposal using the condition technique

Output determination is the process to determine the **"media"** such as printouts, telexes, faxes, e-mails, or EDI that are sent from one business to any of its business partners.

The output can be sent to the business partners (Customer / Vendor) in the format which is defined in documents such as invoices, order confirmations, delivery notes, or shipping notifications. Output determination can be maintained in two ways-

1. Customer master – Output determination can be maintained in customer master. Output proposal triggered by the customer master does not have the benefit of using

an access sequence (A search criteria, which is using to get valid data for a condition type).

2. Condition technique – Output determination can be triggered by condition technique.

Output determination using condition technique can be maintained for three purposes-

- Output determination for sales activities (Sales call, Sales Letter, Phone calls etc.).

- Output determination for sales documents (Invoice, etc.).

- Output determination for billing documents(Billing, etc.).

Output determination for sales activities.

Step 1)

1. Enter T-code V/30 in the command field.

2. Select output types node.

3. Click on new entries' button.

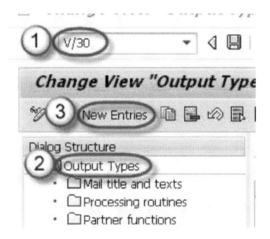

Step 2)

1. Enter output type , description and select general data tab.

2. Enter Access sequence.

3. Check Access to conditions.

4. Unchecked multiple issuing.

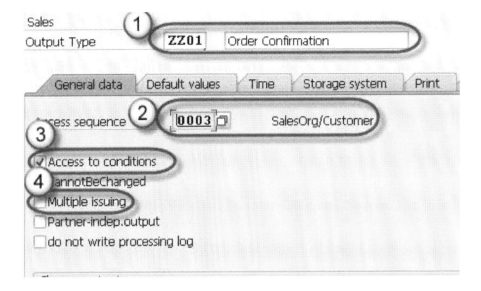

Step 3)

1. Enter Transmission medium(medium of output).

2. Enter Partner function.

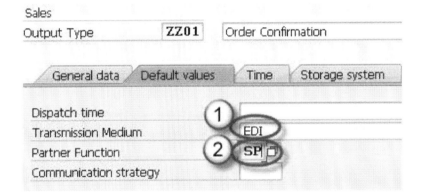

Step 4)

Check timing 4 in time tab.

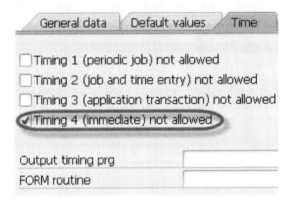

Step 5)

Click on save button. A message "Data was saved " will be displayed.

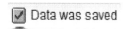

Chapter 25: Substituting Reason

Substituting Reason is a process that controls, how the system performs product selection.

Substitution reason is needed when material substitution action taken place. It defines below things -

- Define strategy for alternate material that should be offered.

- Provide a message for information to user before substitute the material.

Step 1)

1. Enter T-code OVRQ in the command field.

2. Click on New Entries button

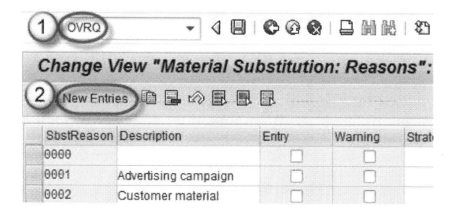

Step 2)

1. Enter Substitute Reason and description.

2. Click on save button.

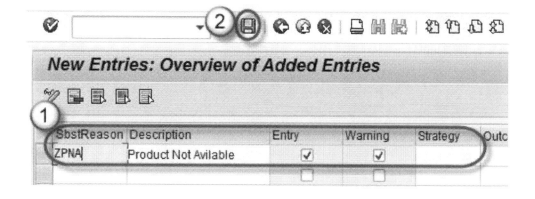

A message "Data was saved " will be displayed.

Chapter 26: How to Create Bill of Materials

A bill of material (BOM) describes the different components that together create a product. For example- A computer is a product. It is a combination of CPU, Keyboard, Monitor, Mouse etc. The bill of material contains the item number of each component, quantity required in the manufacture of a product and the unit of measure of the item.

SAP R/3 allows the creation of various categories of Bill of Material. Some of the categories of the BOM are -

- **Material BOM (T-code CS01)** - A bill of material that you create for a material known as material BOM.

- **Equipment BOM (T-code-IB01) -** Equipement BOM is used to describe the structure of equipment and to assign spare parts to equipment for maintenance purpose.

- **Sales Order BOM (T-code-CS61) -**Sales Order BOM is used for make-to-order production of products according to the requirements of customers.

- **Functional location BOM (T-Code-IB11)** - A functional location BOM can be created individually for each functional location or a group of technical objects.

- **Document BOM (T-code-CS11)** - A complex document may be made up from multiple documents such as program, papers, technical drawing etc. These related information and documentation object grouped as a unit using a BOM.

Step 1) Create Material BOM

1. Enter T-code CS01 in the command field.

2. Enter Material / Plant / BOM usage .

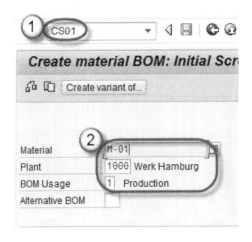

Step 2)

Enter Item Code, Material component and Quanity.

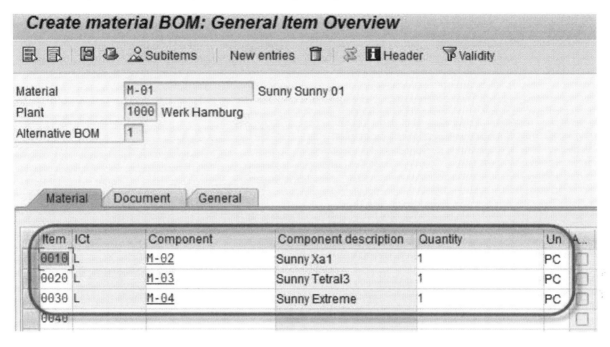

Step 3)

Click on save button. A Message as ☑ Creating BOM for material M-01 will be displayed.

Chapter 27: How to Correct Invoice

What is Invoice Correction?

Invoice Correction is a process to correct quantity or prices in the invoices for one or more line items.

The system calculates the differences between original amount and corrected amount. Invoice correction request is automatically blocked by the system,until it has been checked. Once its approved,we can remove the block.

The system creates either a credit or a debit memo according to the total value of the invoice correction request.

Step 1)

1. Enter T-code VA01 in command field.

2. Enter in Order Type field Invoice Correction Request.

3. Enter Sales Organization / Distribution channel / division in organization data.

4. Click on Create with references button ,to create invoice correction with reference of sales document.

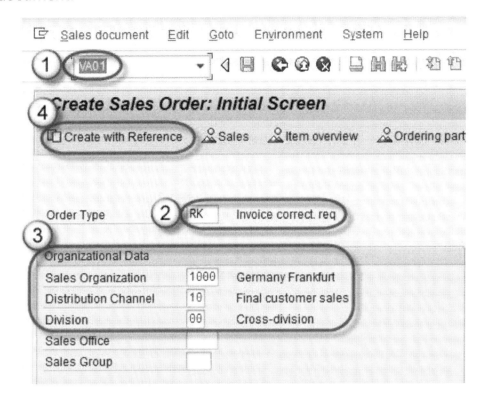

Step 2)

1. Enter Sales order no in which correction is required

2. Click on Copy button.

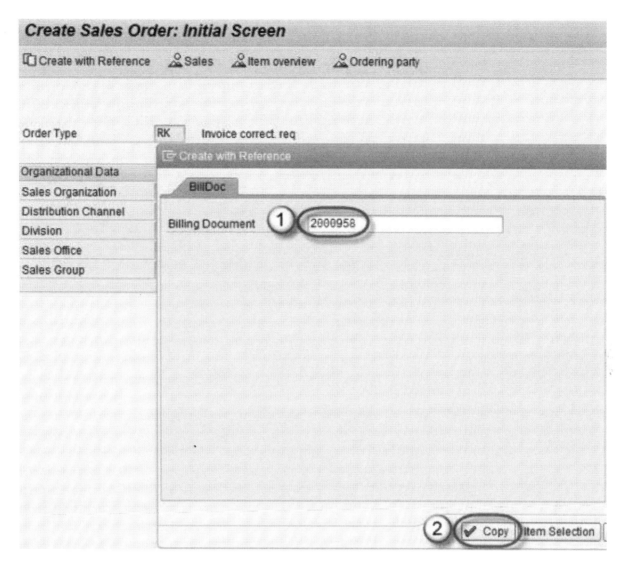

Step 3)

1. Ship-To party / PO Number can be changed.

2. Enter Req. deliv date

3. Order quantity can be changed.

4. Click on save Button.

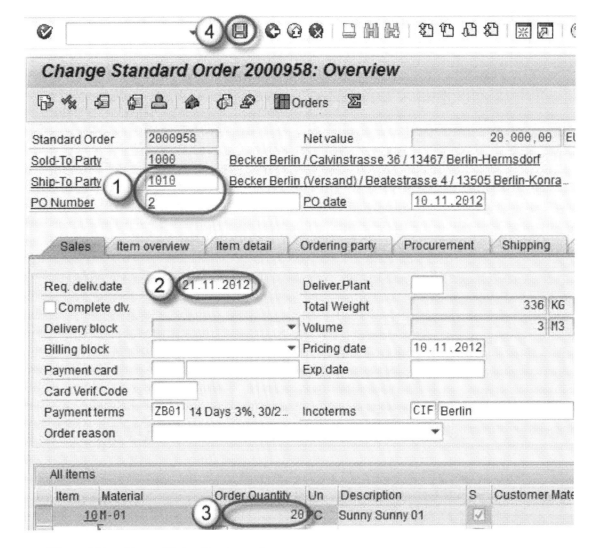

A message "Data Was Saved" is displayed.

Chapter 28: How to Define Item Category

What is Item Category?

An item category defines how a line item behaves in sales transaction.

SAP Uses Item category to process a material differently in each sales document type.

e.g.

AFX - It is inquiry Item category ,it is not relevant for billing.

AGX – It is quotation Item category ,it is not relevant for billing.

TAN – It is standard Item category, it is relevant for billing.

T-code for Define Item category is VOV7.

Step 1)

1. Enter Tcode VOV7 in Command Bar.

2. List of Item Category including SAP and User Define Item category.

3. Click on New Entries New Entries Button,for create Item Category.

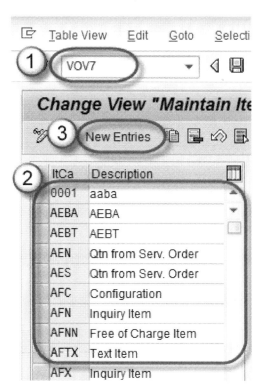

Step 2) While you create new Item category , following sections could be filled.

1. Business Data (billing / pricing etc. information).

2. General Control (It determine automatic batch,rounding permission and order quantity to 1 or not).

3. Transaction Flow(Item screen detail).

4. Bill of Material (used for variant configuration).

5. Value Contract (for value contract).

6. Service Management (service scenario).

7. Control of resource(resource related billing scenario).

We will enter data in Business Data Section.

Sales Document Type	ZSA0 Sales Order	
SD document categ.	C	Sales document block
Indicator		

① Number systems

No.range int.assgt.	01	Item no.increment	10
No. range ext. assg.	02	Sub-item increment	1

② General control

Reference mandatory		Material entry type	
Check division		☑ Item division	
Probability	0	☑ Read info record	
Check credit limit	D	Check purch.order no	
Credit group	01	☐ Enter PO number	
Output application	V1	Commitment date	

③ Transaction flow

Screen sequence grp.	AU Sales Order	Display Range	UALL
Incompl . proced .		FCode for overv.scr.	UER1
Transaction group	0 Sales order	Quotation messages	B
Doc. pric. procedure	A	Outline agrmt mess.	B
Status profile		Message: Mast.contr.	
Alt.sales doc. type1		ProdAttr.messages	
Alt.sales doc. type2		☐ Incomplet.messages	
Variant			

④ Scheduling Agreement

Corr.delivery type		Delivery block	
Usage			
MRP for DlvSchType			

⑤ Shipping

Delivery type	LF Delivery	Immediate delivery	
Delivery block			
Shipping conditions			
ShipCostInfoProfile	STANDARD	Standard freight information	

⑥ Billing

Dlv-rel.billing type		CndType line items	
Order-rel.bill.type		Billing plan type	
Intercomp.bill.type		Paymt guarant. proc.	
Billing block		Paymt card plan type	
		Checking group	

⑦ Requested delivery date/pricing date/purchase order date

Lead time in days		☐ Propose deliv.date	
Date type		☐ Propose PO date	
Prop.f.pricing date			
Prop.valid-from date			

⑧ Contract

PricProcCondHeadr		Contract data allwd.	
PricProcCondItem		FollUpActivityType	
Contract profile		Subseq.order type	
Billing request		Check partner auth.	
Group Ref. Procedure		☐ Update low.lev.cont.	

⑨ Availability check

Business transaction	

Step 3)

1. We are going to create YTA2 (Standard item category)

2. Enter Billing Relevance / Pricing. Check

- Business Item

- Sched. Line Allowed

- Wght

- Vol. Relevant

- Credit Active

- Determine Cost.

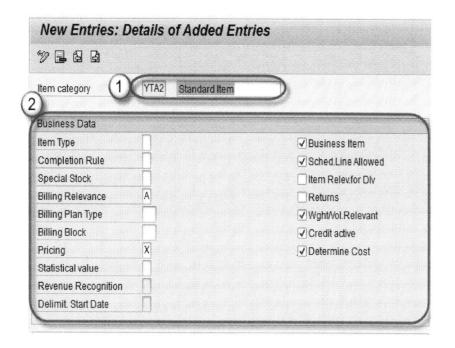

Step 4)

Click On Save ▯ Button.

A Message "Data Was saved " Displayed.

Chapter 29: Steps To Create Blocking Reason

What is Blocking Reason?

Blocking reason is using to block bill creation for a customer. Blocking reason can be defined as per business requirements. After the creation of blocking reason, it has assigned to corresponding document types and used in document processing. Customer can also be blocked in Customer Master.

There are multiple reasons to block customer, some reasons are as below-

- Customer is blacklist due to involvement in unlawful activities.

- Customer defaulted payment.

Blocking is a 2 step process -

1. Create Blocking Reason

2. Assign Blocking Reason

Lets look at these steps in detail-

Step 1) Create Blocking Reason

Step 1.1)

1. Enter T-code S_ALR_87007670 in the command field.

2. Click on choose button.

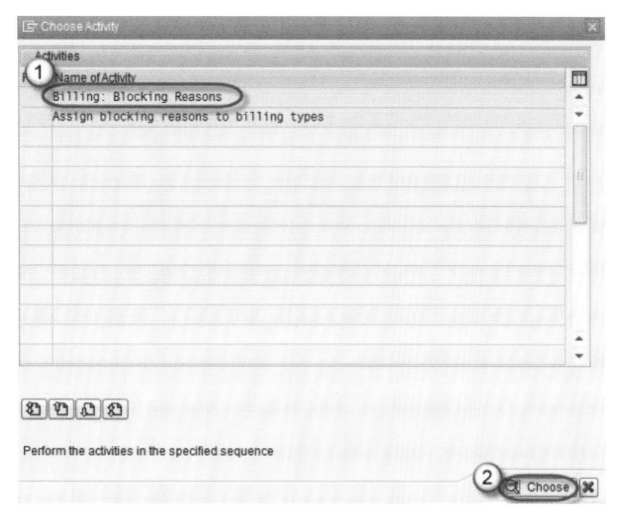

Step 1.2)

- Click on new entries button.

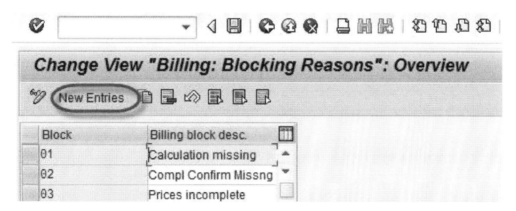

Step 1.3)

1. Enter block code and billing block description.

2. Click on save button.

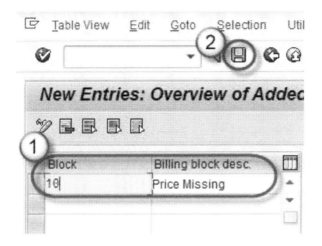

Step 1.4)

Click on save  button.

A message " Data was saved " will be displayed.

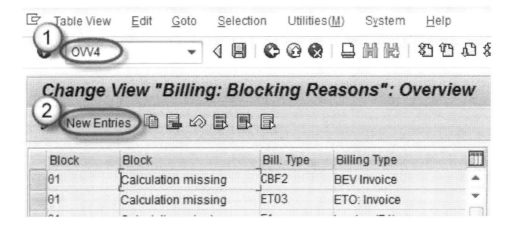

Step 2) Assign Blocking Reason

Step 2.1)

1. Enter T-code OVV4 in command field.

2. Click on new entries button.

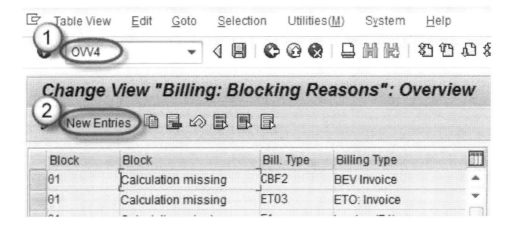

Step 2.2)

1. Enter Blocking code.

2. Enter Billing type.

3. Save the record.

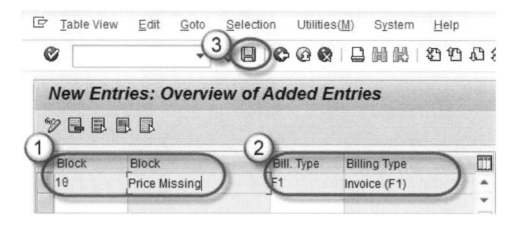

Step 2.3)

A message " Data was saved " displayed.

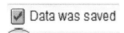

Chapter 30: Determine Pricing by item category

Not all items are relevant for pricing. The standard requirement in pricing procedure checks if the item is relevant for pricing . If this switch in the item category is set to blank, then the line items will not be relevant for pricing.

An item category controls the overall behavior of an item. Item category describes below point-

1. The item is pricing relevant or not.

2. Is item relevant for delivery or not.

3. Is item relevant for billing or not.

4. Is it a free item, text item .

5. It also help to determine the sales document type.

Step 1)

- Enter Tcode OVKO in command field.

- Enter Pricing flag in pricing field.

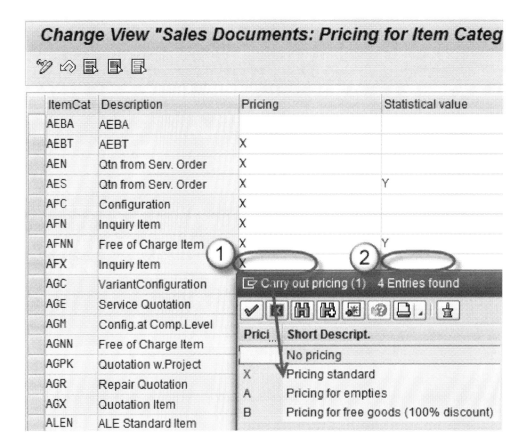

Step 2)

Enter Statistical value Blank,X,Y. Statistical Value flag control an item in the sales documents in three ways-

1. Copy item to header totals.

2. No cumulation - values cannot be used for statistical purposes (item value will not copied into header totals)

3. No cumulation - values can be used for statistical purposes (item value will not copied into header totals)

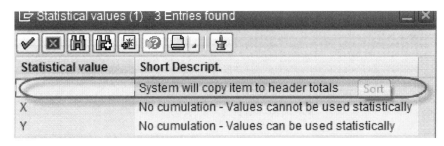

Step 3)

Click on Save 🖫 Button.

Chapter 31: All About Tax Determination Procedure

SAP uses Condition Method technique to calculate taxes (except Withholding Tax) in the system. Tax Calculation Procedures (defined in the system) together with the Tax Codes are used in calculating the amount of tax.

The Tax Code is the first step in the tax calculation procedure. The Tax code describes following -

- **Tax type** (Tax Type can be defined by T-code –OVK1).

- **Amount** of tax calculated / entered.

- **GL account** for tax posting.

- Calculation of **additional tax**.

Each country has a specific Tax Procedure defined in the standard system. A Tax calculation procedure contains the following fields:

- **Steps**— It determine the sequence of lines within the procedure.

- **Condition Types**— Indicates how the tax calculation model will work (whether the records are for fixed amount or percentages and whether the records can be processed automatically.)

- **Reference Steps**— System obtains the amount/value it uses in its calculation (e.g. the base amount).

- **Account/Process Keys**— Provide the link between the tax procedure and the GL accounts to which tax data is to be posted. This helps in automatic tax account assignments. To enable this automatic assignment, there is a need to define the following:

  - **Posting keys** (unless there is a specific requirement, it will be sufficient to use the GL posting keys: Debit: 40, Credit: 50).

  - **Rules** to determine on which fields the account determination is to be based (such as the tax code or country key).

Step 1) Tax Category

Tax Category is used to group and manage similar product tax rates or service tax rates. Tax Rates are defined for each of the tax codes. The tax rates are linked to Tax Types and are included in the tax procedures (in this relationship, it is technically possible that a single tax code can have multiple tax rates for various tax types.) The tax code is assigned to a Tax Procedure, which attaches to a GL master record. A specific tax procedure is accessed whenever that GL account is used in document processing. **Step-1.1**

1. Enter T-code OVK3 in the command field .

2. Click on New Entries Button.

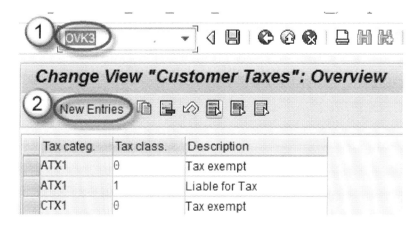

Step 1.2

1. Enter Tax Categories ,Tax class and description.

2. Click on save button.

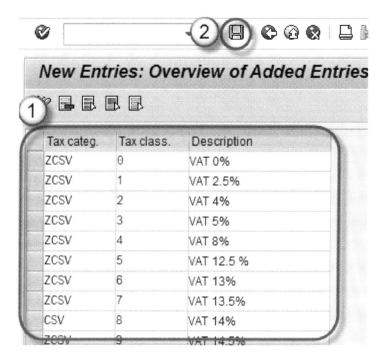

A Message "Data was saved " is displayed.

Step 2) Define Tax Types

Step 2.1

1. Enter T-code - OVK1 in the command field.

2. Click on new entries button.

Step 2.2 Enter Tax country / Sequence / tax category and save the data .

Step 3) Assign the plant for Tax Determination.

Step 3.1

1. Enter T-code OX10 in the command field.

2. Click on New entries Button.

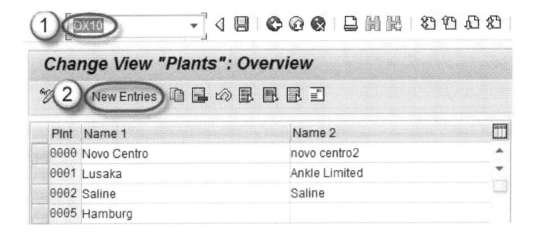

Step 3.2

1. Enter Plant / Name1.

2. Enter country code / city code.

Save the data.

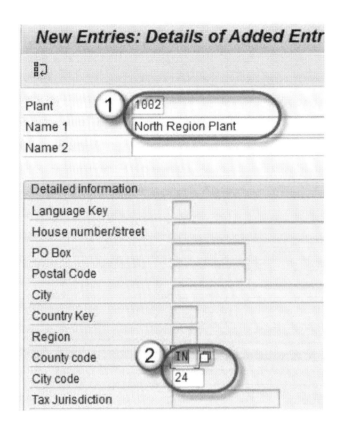

Step 4 Define the Material Taxes.

1. Enter T-code OVK4 in the command field.

2. Click on New Entries Button.

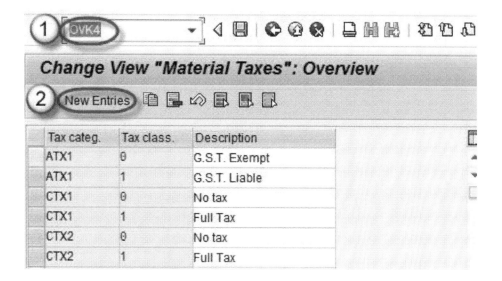

Step 4.1

- Enter Tax category / Tax classification and description.
- Save the data.

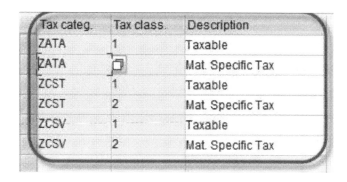

Step 5 Define the Tax Determination

Step 5.1

1. Enter T-code VK12 in the command field.
2. Enter condition type .

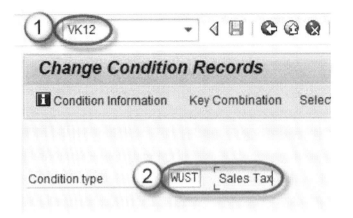

Step 5.2 Select Domestic taxes.

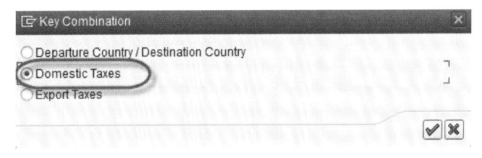

Step 5.3

1. Enter Country / customer tax class / material tax class.

2. Run the report.

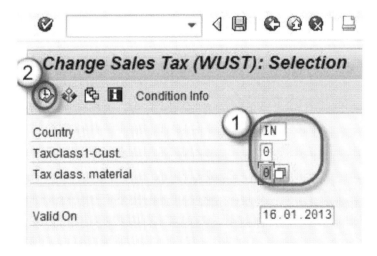

Step 5.4

Enter Customer Tax class/Material Tax class / amount / validity period and tax code.

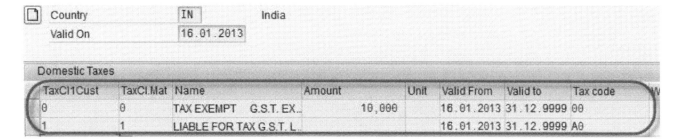

Save the record.

Chapter 32: All about Text Type

What is Text Type?

Text is a small piece of formatted or unformatted text that is used to show or store information in Master data and Transaction data. For example, a temperature sensitive material (a medicine which needs low temperature storage area) needs to be kept under freezing temperature. One can configure a text field in Sales Document with specific comments such that on sale of any such product , customer is informed to to store the medicine in refrigeration. This Text is known as "**Material Sales Text**".

Text Types

Each text item ("Material Sales Text") in the example above is called a **Text Type**. It internally contains a **Text ID**. These are configured in the *Text Types* section. Text can be defined for-

- Customer

- Sales document

- Delivery

- Billing

Step 1)

1. Enter T-code VOTXN in command field.

2. Select sales & distribution radio button of customer block.

3. Click on change button.

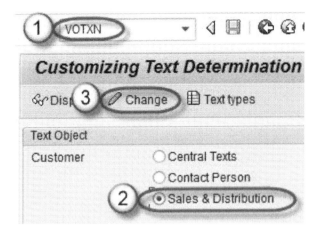

Step 2)

1. Select text procedure node.

2. Click on New Entries button.

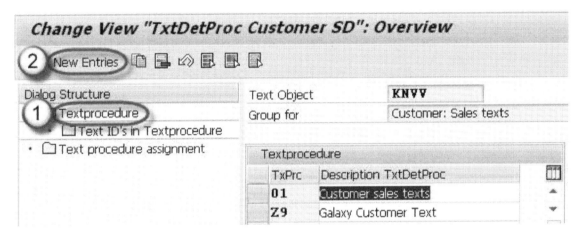

Step 3)

1. Select text-procedure node.

2. Enter Text-procedure and its description.

3. Click on save button.

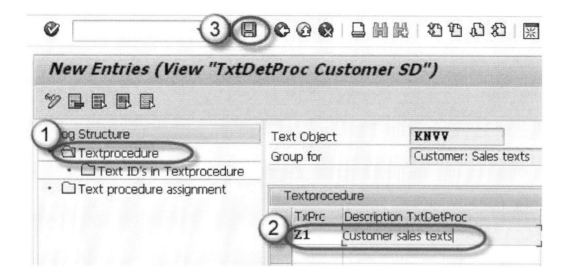

Step 4)

1. Select Text Id's in text-procedure node.

2. Enter SeqNo / ID / ID description.

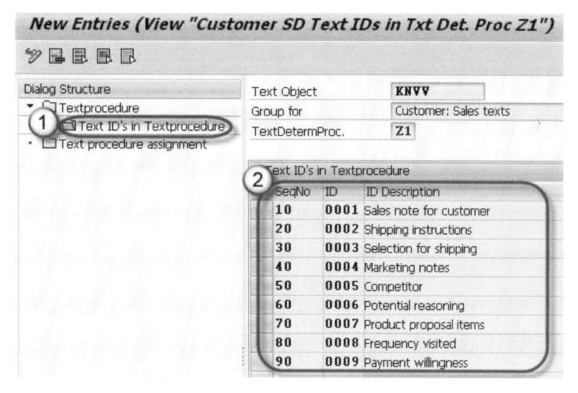

Step 5)

1. Select Text procedure assignment.

2. Assign text procedure to customer account group.

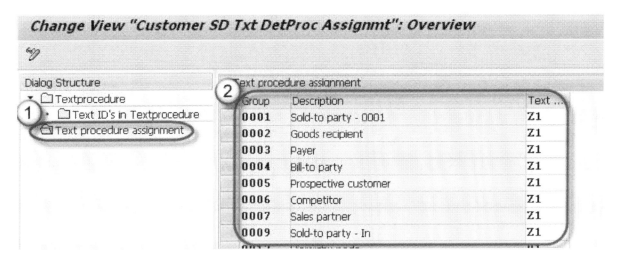

Step 6)

Click on save button. A message "Data was saved" will be displayed.

Chapter 33: SAP Item Category Determination: VOV7, VOV4

Item category controls the item behavior .e.g. Item category define that item is relevant for Billing or Pricing.

The item category in the sales document depends on the sales document type and the material.

Item Category Determination is done by T-code –VOV4. There are Many Standard Item Categories provide by SAP, Some of them is below-

Item Categories	Description
TAN	Standard Item
TAB	Individual Purchase Order
TAS	Third Party Item

TAD	Service
TATX	Text Item
TANN	Free Of Charge
AFX	Inquiry Item
AGX	Quotation Item

Step 1)

1. Enter T-code VOV4 in Command Field.

2. A list of existing item category displayed.

3. To Create a New item category click on New Entries New Entries Button.

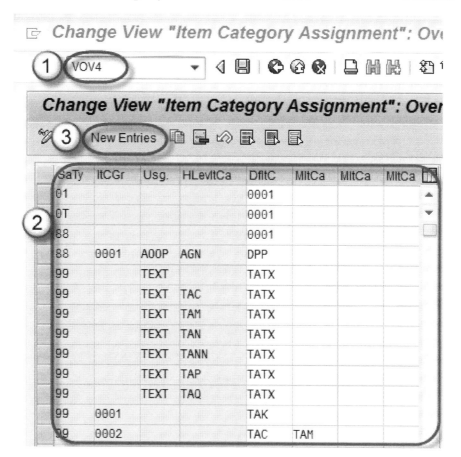

Step 2)

To Create New Item Category ,Enter following data   -

- Sales Doc. type.

- Item cat. group.

- Item category (Default item category,this can be overridden with manual item category value).

- Manual item category (if business demands,we can add manual item category to override default item category).

 Note :   Default item category will be picked up automatically for sales document type in which it's define. Manual Item Category can be used in place of default item category OR we can replace default item category in sales document with allowed manual item category. e.g. Default item category(YTA2) can be replaced with Manual item category (TAP,TAQ,TANN).

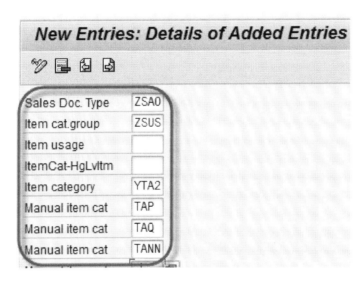

Step 3)

Click on Save 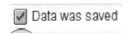 Button.

A Message "Data Was Saved " displayed as below -

✓ Data was saved

Chapter 34: All About Condition Exclusion Group

What is Condition Exclusion Group?

In any normal situation there could be more than one condition type in a pricing procedure offering a discount to a customer. Should the discounts be automatically determined, there is the risk that the customer will receive all the relevant discounts and thus purchase the product for a lower price than he should.

By using 'condition exclusion groups' you can ensure that the customer does not receive all the discounts, but instead only receives the best of the available discount condition types.

T-code-OV31.

Step 1)

1. Enter T-code OV31 in command field.

2. Click on New Entries button.

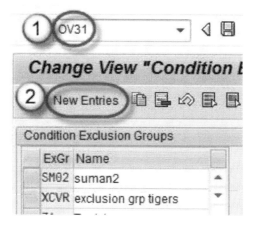

Step 2)

1. Enter Condition exclusion group code and name.

2. Click on save button.

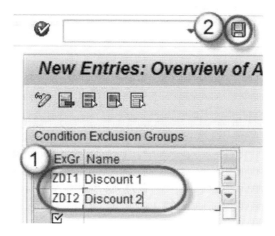

A message "Data was saved " will be displayed.

Assign Condition Types to Exclusion Group

.

Step 1)

1. Enter T-code OV32 in command field.
2. Click on New Entries Button.

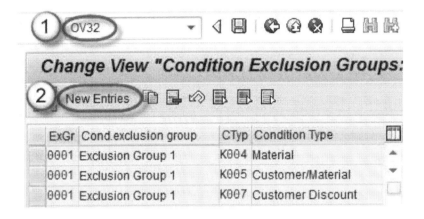

Step 2)

1. Assign Exclusion group to Condition type.
2. Click on save button.

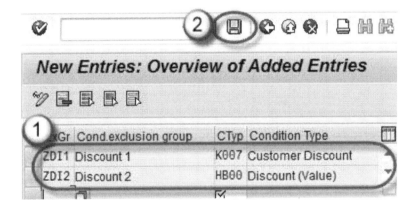

Assign Exclusion group to Procedure.

Step 1)

1. Enter T-code VOK8 in command field.
2. Select Procedure .
3. Select Exclusion Node.

4. Click on save button.

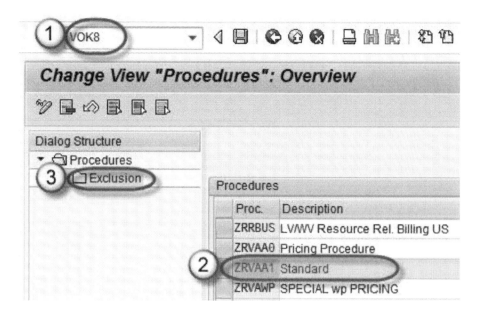

Step 2)

There are 7 condition exclusion groups available as below:

A: Best condition between condition types

B: Best condition within the condition type

C: Best condition between two exclusion groups

D: Exclusive

E: Least favorable within the condition type

F: Least favorable between the two exclusion groups

L: Least favorable between condition types

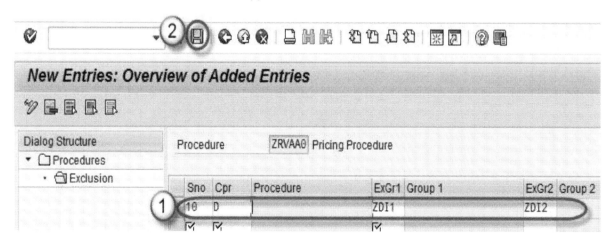

When you set up the exclusion group as above, when you create an order in VA01 the condition K007 gets deactivated when user enters value for condition .

Chapter 35: Accounting Key

What is Accounting Key?

A condition type writes its value to a key established in the configuration outside the pricing procedure. That key is called the Account Key, which is a table entry that tells the pricing procedure where to copy calculated condition values.

The Accounting key enables the system to post amounts to certain types of revenue account. For example, the system can post freight charges (generated by the freight pricing condition) to the relevant freight revenue account.

Step 1) Creating Accounting Key

1. Enter T-code OV34 in command field.

2. Click on New Entries button.

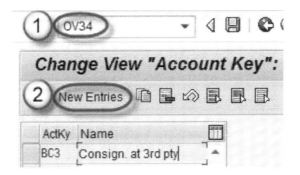

Step 2)

1. Enter Accounting key and name.

2. Click on save button.

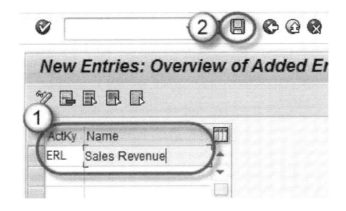

A message "Data was saved" will be displayed.

Chapter 36: Guide to Credit Management in SAP

Credit Management is a process in which Company sells a product / service to customers on credit basis. The company collects payments from customer at a later time , after sale of product. The amount of credit fixed by a company for a customer is called **credit limit**. The customer can Purchase the product from a company within the credit limit, and when the credit limit is crossed, order is blocked by the system.

Example- Consider a Company creates a credit limit for Customer of 200,000. Customer can purchase the product from the company on credit till the credit limit 200,000 is reached.Customer gives an Order # 1 of amount 100000. Again Customer gives an Order # 2 of the amount 1,50000. Now, the total open order crosses credit limit of a customer.Order 2 is blocked by the system due to credit limit reached.

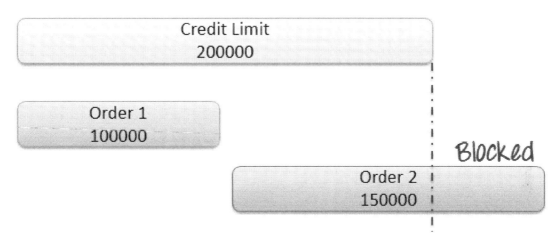

Here customer ordered a total of Rs. 2,50,000,while a customer credit limit is Rs. 2,00,000.Here order 2 is over to the credit limit of a customer. So the order 2 will be blocked by the system.Credit limit can be different for each customer .

Types of credit checks:

1. **Simple credit check:** Simple Credit Check = Value of all Open Items + Value of the Current Sales Order. Note: Open Items are invoices for which company has not received payment.

 2. **Automatic Credit check** - Automatic credit check allows you to evaluate a transaction based on the credit rating of the customer, and ensures appropriate further processing of the transaction document. The credit limit check starts either automatically when you save a document or by selecting Check Credit. Automatic credit checks are of 2 types-

1. Static Credit Check (Check for credit limit against total value of open sales order + open delivery not invoiced + billing value of open billing document not passed at accounting).

2. Dynamic Credit Check (Check for credit limit against open sales order not yet delivered + open delivery not invoiced + billing value of open billing document not passed at accounting + passed but not paid bill amount).

Step 1) Set Credit Check

1. Enter T-code OVA8 in command field.

2. Click On New Entries button.

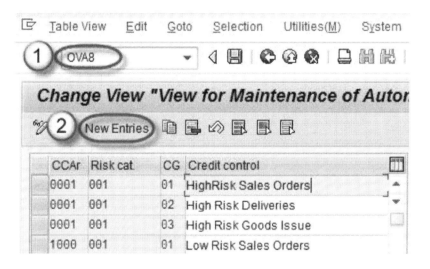

Step 2)

1. Enter Credit Control.

2. Check credit Check option.

3. Enter Credit limit validity period.

4. Check Static option .

5. Check open orders and deliveries.

Change View "View for Maintenance of Automatic Credit Control":

New Entries

1 RkC CG Credit control   Curr.   Update
0001 001 01 HighRisk Sales Orders   EUR   000012

Document controlling   Released documents are still unchecked

2 credit check   Deviation in %
✓ Item check   Number of days

3 edit limit seasonal factor   Checks in financial accounting/old A/R summary
        From   To   ☐ Payer
2   ☐ Minus 23.12.2012 23.01.2013   Permitted days   Permitted hours

Checks

4   Reaction Status **5** ck
✓ Static   A   ✓   ✓ Open orders   ✓ Open deliveries
☐ Dynamic   Horizon   2 T
☐ Document value   Max.doc.value

Step 3)

Click on save Button.